THE VOICE OF GOD PROJECT

Copyright © 2017 by Charles Brandon Wagoner

All rights reserved. This book or any portion thereof may not be reproduced or used in any manner whatsoever without the express written permission of the publisher except for the use of brief quotations in a book review or scholarly journal.

First Printing: 2017

All Scripture quotations, unless otherwise indicated, are taken from the Holy Bible, New International Version®, NIV®. Copyright © 1973, 1978, 1984, 2011 by Biblica, Inc.™ Used by permission of Zondervan. All rights reserved worldwide. www.zondervan.com The "NIV" and "New International Version" are trademarks registered in the United States Patent and Trademark Office by Biblica, Inc.™

Scripture quotations marked MSG are taken from *THE MESSAGE*, copyright © 1993, 1994, 1995, 1996, 2000, 2001, 2002 by Eugene H. Peterson. Used by permission of NavPress. All rights reserved. Represented by Tyndale House Publishers, Inc.

ISBN-13: 978-0-9990716-0-1 (Paperback edition)
ISBN-13: 978-0-9990716-1-8 (Hardcover edition)
ISBN-13: 978-0-9990716-2-5 (eBook edition)

LCCN: 2017949619

For more information about this or other Grassleaf works, please visit grassleafpublishing.com or email info@grassleafpublishing.com.

A note about Grassleaf Publishing

I created Grassleaf Publishing because I believe good literary works, films, music, and art of all types can come from anywhere and anyone. After all, all goodness comes from He who created goodness, and He is powerful enough to display that goodness through any individual.

As my writing turned from a personal hobby into a passion, I quickly learned that I had no chance to see my work be published without a platform with thousands of followers. This was disappointing as a writer, but also disheartening as a reader. What kind of good works am I missing out on?

So, a new calling developed for me, and instead of trying to coax agents and publishers into publishing my books, I decided to start my own publishing company.

Publishers will tell us that people do not read anymore. They blame the old-fashioned, boring art of reading. However, when one inspects the quality of books being printed, it is easy to see why consumers have turned away. Books are published based on the name of the author, not the quality of the content. Occasionally, a good book will make its way through, and readers will devour it over a weekend...especially young readers. So, it isn't the art of reading that's old-fashioned.

At Grassleaf Publishing, it is believed that good books can still be written. But the process of publishing must evolve. That's why Grassleaf operates differently than the traditional publishing company. Content and quality are the sole focus. The status, background, or life experience of an author doesn't matter. Grassleaf Publishing believes that if good content is made available, He will see that it serves its purpose.

As a reader, you may not recognize Grassleaf's authors, but hopefully you will recognize our logo and trust that it represents a worthwhile work.

Grassleaf Publishing was created to do one thing: contribute a verse.

– Charles Brandon Wagoner

THE VOICE OF GOD PROJECT

C. Brandon Wagoner

For Sarah,
my clearest reminder of God's goodness in 2016.

Introduction

What follows in these pages is a journal that I wrote throughout 2016. I started the journal as a way to document my own spiritual journey. Previously, I got into the habit of writing my own reviews and conclusions of books that I read, and I loved going back and reading those thoughts from time to time. So, when I got the idea to complete a spiritual journey by reading books from authors of various backgrounds, I knew part of the process would involve me recording my thoughts of each work. Therefore, I decided to get a journal dedicated to this year of spiritual journey.

But I had no idea what kind of year 2016 was going to be.

Tragedies were rampant, violence was prevalent, division and hatred seemed to be at a level I had not before experienced in my lifetime. At the outset, I was hoping the books that I was reading would help me learn more about God's Spirit and the world He created, but every day the world seemed to throw questions at me faster than I could find answers. And as the year progressed, the bulk of my writing centered less around the works I was reading and more around current events.

I began to consistently ask myself how a Christ Follower is supposed to live in today's culture. How do we accurately show our faith? When the world seems to be two sides fighting against each other all the time, where do we fit? When there is no clear right or wrong sometimes, how do we respond? Avoidance? Engagement? To what level?

This book is a peek into my mind as I've wrestled with these questions. I started this journey out with the fruit of the Spirit as my lens into God's character, and I shouldn't have been surprised to find that it was precisely those nine traits that helped me to see the key to relevancy of faith in the twenty-first century.

Do you know what the scariest part of writing a book like this is? The fact that these are my current thoughts and that there is a chance my thoughts will change over time. In fact, I think differently about a variety of topics today than I did ten years ago, yet my name will always be on this work. For that, I ask for grace. I ask for those of you who take the time to actually read these words to listen for my heart and to give me some benefit of the doubt in questionable situations.

The point of this book is not to tell everyone the right way to think about things. My goal is to show my posture of trying to learn over the year and to share what I believe I've learned with others in case there is some benefit.

Perhaps you could say this book is really one long prayer as I have sought God's wisdom and tried to lay my concerns at His feet.

I have taken some liberty with the writing of my journal into a book. I have restructured a few events so that the flow is better for reading. I noticed some common themes, and I tried to group them together for a better reader experience.

As you read, you will be introduced to people in my life who made an impact on me throughout this specific year, and I will also reference the books I read. However, I have made no attempt to overtly describe these people or the characters of the books. I know that this may take away from the reader's experience, and that the reader may even feel lost at times. But I believe that providing more description adds negligible value to the work as a whole, and it may even cause more confusion in some instances. I would recommend every work that is cited in this book, and you can find all the appropriate bibliography information on any of these works in the Notes section.

Finally, I want to make a comment about the dreams mentioned in this book. I wrote about two different dreams that I had during the year, one of which was recurring. I know they may be hard to believe, but I have written them down as best as I can remember them. No, I did not make these up. I know readers may be skeptical, but I can only tell you the truth. I wish I could make something like that up. It was these dreams that solidified my desire to make this journal into a book.

I hope the words in this book benefit your spiritual life. I consider your time to be valuable, and I thank you for giving me some of this precious resource. I have worked hard in hopes that you will look at the time spent reading this work as worthwhile.

Foreword

Spiritual Journey Eve

The Voice of God Project

12/31/15

I have not looked forward to a New Year's Day quite as much as I have this year. And I have no real resolutions, just more intention to what I'm exposing myself to, which I hope may produce total transformation. It feels like Christmas Eve, that feeling of excitement and anticipation. The only difference is knowing that it won't be over tomorrow. Just beginning. Starting. Starting a journey.

It's beyond exciting to think of where this journey will take me to and through. What will I see? Think? Feel? What will surprise me? What will shape me and how? How will I be different in 365 days? How will I view my 12/31/15 self a year from now?

I guess I have to thank *The River Why*[1] for this idea. In David James Duncan's book, Gus is a young man who lives in solitude next to a river so that he can fish all day every day. I love the idea of Gus separating himself from the world and intentionally seeking a higher power. He had his philosopher friend that challenged him, his trips along the river that forced him to think, and his friend Nick that showed him the conviction of story.

His journey leads him to conviction, and it's enough to make one want to attempt to mimic his experience. But how does one participate in a modern spiritual journey? Particularly one who has a wife, children, full-time job, church obligations, family, and friends? He can't move to a solitary place until he has life figured out.

The fact is I cannot fully disconnect from the world, but I can be intentional about what I expose myself to (physically) and what I feed myself (spiritually). I don't want to shelter myself this year, but I do want to practice solitude, which will require some isolation.

So, before one begins a journey, I believe it is important to know where one wants to arrive. Otherwise, the journey becomes wandering. My original thought was that a spiritual journey should lead to deeper understanding. After all, isn't that what Gus experiences as he feels God's hook set into his heart? However, after some consideration, I now realize that I'm incorrect and that to set understanding as a goal would be to set myself up for failure.

My goal is to take a lesson from Mary in Luke, at the end of Chapter 2. She and Joseph lost track of Jesus, and they frantically traced their steps all the way back to where they had last seen him. After searching for Jesus for three days, Mary arrived at the very last place to look: the temple.

Surely, He wasn't still there. That would mean He had never left. He couldn't have just stayed there for three days as His family left Him. As Mary walked in, full of panic, she had to resist the urge to resign that her son was lost forever.

But there He was! Immediately, she asked Him why He hadn't gone with them. She even expressed her disappointment in Him. Jesus gave her an answer, but the Bible says she couldn't understand what He was saying to her and Joseph.

That always seemed weird to me for several reasons: 1) the answer Jesus gave wasn't that complex; 2) it is written as if she couldn't understand the words themselves; and 3) why would the writer include such a trivial comment?

Perhaps the writer included it to make a bigger point. Searching for Jesus doesn't mean that when we find Him, we're also going to find understanding. Our 'why' questions may not be answered, at least to our satisfaction. But we will find something else that is even better than understanding.

The very next verse states, "...his mother treasured all these things in her heart" (Luke 2:51).

Can you imagine the relief and peace she must have felt when she saw her son? Finding Jesus isn't guaranteeing that we'll also find answers or understanding. But I believe we will find peace. And upon further inspection, I believe this is what Gus actually embraces at the end of his journey.

Peace is my 2016 destination.

But back to the original question: how does one go on a spiritual journey in today's world with today's responsibilities? Well, I have an idea for a project. I guess you could call it an experiment, but being an engineer, I work in projects, not so much in experiments. But maybe this is both. A project in the sense that I know what I want to achieve, but an experiment in the sense of how I'm going to try to achieve it.

My project is: I want to hear the Voice of God.

And that's why I need to somehow isolate myself from other voices this year. I can't quit my job and go trekking through the mountains. But I can be intentional about listening and about who I'm listening to.

My experiment: I want to hear the Voice of God from a variety of resources, from people of all different backgrounds, from people who may not even know they are transmitting the Voice of God.

The next step is setting out some criteria. I am aware of the concept that the Spirit bears fruit. My question is how to evaluate what will bear this fruit? In an attempt to answer that question, I have come up with the following criteria: I will evaluate one book each month that I believe will bear the fruit of love, joy, peace, patience, kindness, goodness, faithfulness, gentleness, and/or self-control by its planting into my life. If the resource speaks at least one of these fruits, then I think it is speaking, at least in some way, God's Spirit. And I want to see what I can learn about God's Spirit from people of all walks of life.

I had hoped, at one point, to have my list of resources selected by now. But…how crazy is that? I really only need to know one month ahead. Be that as it may, I have a fairly substantial list going. It will be added to, probably taken away from, too. I don't want to be rigid. Some of these books are quite long (*The Brothers Karamazov*), and I don't want to ignore them because they may not fit in a month. If I only read nine books, so be it. The point is not to rush but quite the opposite: to dwell.

These books will become seeds that I plant into my life throughout the year. This notebook will be my garden journal where I study my fruit and log their growth, where I measure the intangible: transformation.

It is my theory that the fruit of this journey will permeate all aspects of my life.

While right now I do not know what books I will consume, I do know that I have a few rules in their selection:

1) No double authors. I will not read the same author twice as I do not want to follow man but God. This is the Voice of God Project, not the Voice of Man Project.
2) I want a mixture of non-fiction and literature – the parable of the modern day.

I believe there are three types of books: 1) non-fiction, 2) fiction that is a story for the sake of a story (Stephen King, Michael Connelly), and 3) fiction that makes you think, evaluate, grow – what I call literature (Harper Lee, Ernest Hemingway). Perhaps Solomon was the first literary author as he wrote Ecclesiastes. This third type of book will be my main focus, though I will also dive into some non-fiction. As much as I love a good story and admire the works of good storytellers, I will probably avoid the second type this year.

To me, Jesus's parables were examples of literature. They are these wonderful stories that speak to the deepest part of us, the soul that was created by the Creator. I think they are evidence of a creator. He starts out with, "The Kingdom of God is like...", and then He follows that with a story that makes sense to us deep down at our core, regardless of our background, education level, familiarity with scripture. There is something in us that these parables speak to, something that responds by saying, "Yes! That is good! That is right!" When we hear about the son who doesn't deserve forgiveness, but his father not only forgives him but also throws him a party (Luke 15:11-32) – that gives us joy. We long for that. Our soul recognizes that and yearns for it. How can we hear these stories and walk away not knowing we were created?

Think about this. In the New Testament, Jesus references scripture at times but not always. When He finds Himself around people who are familiar with scripture, He communicates with them using scripture. However, when He finds Himself around crowds or people less familiar with scripture, He communicates with them using parables. Analogies. Fictional stories. Literature. He makes this great point that anyone can understand the complexity of God's Kingdom regardless of their knowledge of scripture. He meets people exactly where they are and speaks in a language they feel comfortable with. He uses seemingly non-spiritual activities in non-spiritual stories to make profoundly spiritual impacts.

I believe literature is the modern-day parable and speaks to that same part of us, and that is why I'm eager to see what I can learn about my Creator from them.

I want a diverse background of authors: Ann Voskamp, Fyodor Dostoevsky, Robert M. Pirsig, Yann Martel. I don't expect to agree with all of them or even enjoy some of them, but I want this year to maintain a posture of listening without the ability to rebut (fruit of patience and self-control). That's the whole growth catalyst of reading a book.

Chapter 1

January 2016

The Voice of God Project

1/14/16

Well, I finished my first book, *Jesus, My Father, the CIA, and Me: A Memoir…of Sorts*[1] by Ian Morgan Cron, in just eleven days. At 252 pages, it wasn't a long book, but it certainly wasn't short either. I'd never heard of this book before, nor the writer, but I fell in love with Cron's wit, style, language, and particularly his story. One reason I could lose myself in this book so quickly and so deeply is because I could really relate to him in some ways. The way he felt like a burden to people, the way he tried to get attention by being perfect, the yearning he had for God at such a young age, the way he tries so hard to give his own children a perfect childhood: I have felt (and still feel) all these ways.

A close friend of mine, Wilson, gave me this book as a Christmas gift. He read it a few months ago, and when I told him my idea about a modern spiritual journey, he thought this book would be one to put on my list. And I'm grateful that he did, even though Cron's book (I believe) has had a strange impact on me. I am fairly certain that one (if not both!) of the following events is occurring: 1) Satan does not like my idea of doing a spiritual journey, and has thus decided to launch a full-on attack at me; 2) reading a book that focuses so much on certain relationships has brought to life some raw emotions that haven't been fully processed and even some memories that have apparently been at least partially repressed, and my method of dealing with them has been to distract myself from them and close off all further vulnerabilities.

During this journey, I expected to plant seeds of the Spirit (by reading books) and then sit back and watch the fruit grow. I didn't expect that I would have to also take on the task of weeding the garden lest my vines be choked to death before fruit even has a chance to appear. And how does one weed a spiritual garden, anyway? Obviously, I have determined the objective of the weeds: distraction and retreat. I fight the urge to be distracted or retreat from uncomfortable situations, but it doesn't work.

It feels like being swallowed up by a large blanket and struggling to get out but never being able to. It's like trying to grow fruit in spite of the presence of weeds.

I want to kill the weeds.

To do this, I need to address the weeds head-on by intentionally acting in ways opposite of how I've behaved in the past. Instead of giving in to distraction when I feel the urge to procrastinate and avoid difficult situations, I must embrace them head on. Instead of retreating, I must advance and become more vulnerable, and in the process, open myself up to more potential rejection. This takes time, and I have had NONE. This is not an excuse, but reality. For embrace, I need quiet, which seems to not exist. This journey will be harder than I thought (as my son and daughter are screaming from the other room as I write).

1/18/16

As I ask myself what seeds this book has planted, I have a hard time eliminating some. Isn't love a strong theme throughout Cron's book? The lack of love given him by his father, the love he had a hard time giving to himself, the search for and eventual acceptance of the love God has for him. Joy is just as much a seed of this book as love. Cron, in effect, had sought to reap joy through the planting of various seeds: alcohol, drugs, over-achieving. He did, in fact, enjoy a bountiful harvest of joy by the end of the book, but he had to plant the right seeds for the fruit to grow. This included seeds of forgiveness, grace, mercy, and confession. Eventually, Cron found himself at peace with all that life had given him (from his wonderful, heaven-sent wife to his drunken, narcissistic father). Isn't this peace the goal of life?

I could make a case for at least patience, faithfulness, and goodness, but the first themes are the ones that spoke to me. They are the ones that planted seeds into my life. Love, joy, and peace are the fruits in which I am clearing all weeds that they may grow.

At one point, Cron mentioned that he went to the doctor because he didn't feel well. He didn't know what was wrong, and after he spoke with the doctor and told of his symptoms, the doctor told him that he was waking up[2]. This resonated with me. Maybe it's my age, maybe it's having children, but something in my life has made me more aware, more concerned, more inquisitive.

This book has brought me face to face with the difficult and important questions of life. I feel like I have come to the edge of a cliff and now stand overlooking a gorge. On the other side is beauty and peace, but standing in the way is a deep, dark, intimidating abyss. There's no way to go over the ravine; I must go through it. And while it is tempting to turn back, Cron has shown me that it is worth it to press on. He has taught me there is meaning found in the abyss.

So, I ask myself the questions I must if I want to move forward.

Love: Do I really believe I am loved? Do I even allow myself to be loved by God? I'm really not sure. God knows me better than anyone. Perhaps, I believe He feels the same way about me that I feel about myself: a fake, a phony. Oh, I think I know that He loves me, but sometimes I want to feel special to Him. This goes back to Cron's attempts at standing out because of his perfect behavior. Have I not done the same thing? And in the end, perhaps I can fool everyone else, but I can't fool myself. And I can't fool God. I'm not perfect. Never have been.

Joy: I need to answer this question. It should be the most important thing in my world right now. With all the blessings that surround and permeate my life, why do I not constantly radiate joy? In fact, because of the statement above regarding my consistent imperfection, I should be more joyful because it is obvious that the blessings in my life have not been earned. Instead, the opposite occurs. I feel guilty because I don't deserve that which has been given to me.

Peace: There is probably no point investigating this yet. Until I get the other two figured out, this seems impossible.

1/19/16

I had a dream the other night. It is rare that I remember dreams, and I can probably count on one hand the number of dreams I remember as vividly as this one. As soon as I woke up, I had the clear realization that this dream undeniably had a meaning. It was more like a parable spoken straight from Christ than a movie playing in my head while I slept. It's one thing to know your dream had meaning; it's a completely different thing to know what that meaning is, which was obvious to me immediately.

I was going golfing with three friends: Wilson, Nathan, and Will. When we arrived, everyone was ready to play…everyone except me. For whatever reason, I had not dressed in my golf attire. So, while the other guys decided to split a bucket of range balls, I headed to the locker room. I took my time getting dressed. Then, I decided to get a bite to eat and a cup of coffee. After that, I ran into some people I knew and struck up a conversation. I found more and more ways to prolong my time in the clubhouse, but eventually I walked out the back door to see Will kicked back in the driver's seat of our cart. The other two were nowhere to be found. It was obvious Will was very upset, but I was just confused.

Before I had a chance to inquire of the whereabouts of Wilson and Nathan, Will angrily spit a question at me: "Where have you been?" His every word emphasized a tone of disbelief. I opened my mouth to explain, but Will cut me off, indicating his indifference to my response, as no excuse could validate the length of time I kept him waiting. "Wilson and Nathan are gone," he explained with condemnation. "Been gone. They're probably almost done!" In that moment, I realized with regret that I had messed up and missed out. There was nothing I could do to fix things. I just wanted another chance that I knew I wouldn't get. I wanted to go back in time and start over, but that was impossible.

I knew the meaning of this dream immediately. It really ties in quite closely with Cron's book. I, like Cron, have allowed myself to not only get distracted, but pulled in a wrong direction. I have procrastinated. I have put time and energy into things that should be secondary instead of primary, or even eliminated.

I could feel God's message to me in this dream, and I have translated it in this way: "Brandon, do you realize that the time you should have been spending on the links has been spent in the clubhouse? You know you're here for a reason, right? And that reason is not to find ways of passing and wasting time. Furthermore, you know what you're here to do, in the same way that it's not a mystery to someone who drives to a golf course. The game is going to go on with or without you, but you need to decide how long you're going to mess around and miss out."

I feel like this dream was my own call to wake up.

But this scares me. And it's because it has to do with calling. There is something I really, really want to do, but how do I know if it is a calling or just a dream of mine that doesn't really have anything to do with God? If I knew that what I felt passionate about was a calling from God, I'd drop everything I'm currently doing and embrace it. However, if it isn't a calling from God, I'm opening myself up to failure, criticism, ridicule. This is when vulnerability really comes in to play.

1/23/16

It snowed the other day, and since we were snowed in, Julie and I watched Penny Marshall's *Awakenings*. They just don't make movies like they used to. This movie touched me, and I wanted to make a record of that. The scene that spoke the most to my spiritual journey was when Leonard (who had been in a catatonic state for thirty years up to that point!) called Dr. Sayer in the middle of the night because he was just so passionate about life and had the overwhelming urge, the need, to spread his message to someone. He was like all humankind who, at some point in life, wants to grab the world by the tail and set it right. He, in a much more literal sense than Cron and myself, was having his own waking up moment.

> Leonard: We've got to tell them, everybody. We've got to remind them. We've got to remind them how good it is.
> Dr. Sayer: How good what is, Leonard?
> Leonard: Read the newspaper. What does it say? All bad. It's all bad. People have forgotten what life is all about. They've forgotten what it is to be alive. They need to be reminded. They need to be reminded of what they have and what they can lose. What I feel is the joy of life, the gift of life, the freedom of life, the wonderment of life! [3]

That is joy! Why don't I feel that every day? Leonard lost thirty years of his life to his illness. He was stuck inside an institution as he shouted these words into the phone. Why on earth does his life radiate more joy than mine? There is a part of me that begins to doubt a little bit. I mean, if I'm a Christ Follower and one of the fruits of God's Spirit is joy, why don't I radiate this kind of attitude? In fact, my own life looks more filled with impatience, frustration, begrudging, avoidance, and harshness. The dots don't seem to connect.

1/29/16

Last night, Julie and I finished *Dead Poets Society*[4]. What a movie! When was the last time a movie inspired like that? How great and precious is this gift of life! How short and fleeting our time is, and shorter every day! Oh, I groan at how willing we are to allow ourselves to get distracted and even to go out of our way to distract ourselves.

It seems that the only time a human being is willing anymore to be active in life is when the result of that activity reaps the ability to live more passively.

Thoreau said, "The mass of men lead lives of quiet desperation."[5] This movie embraces this unfortunate truth and assigns it the gravity it deserves. Robin Williams was an amazing actor and a fascinating person. I've watched some interviews of him, and I admire his brilliant mind. He was a deep thinker.

The most famous scene of *Dead Poets Society* occurs early, and it plants this little seed that grows and blossoms throughout the entire movie. It's a seed most of us ignore, and when a shoot appears, we immediately rip it out, trying to avoid its presence. It's the seed of mortality.

Mr. Keating makes the boys look at pictures of former students that have long passed away. He puts them in the shoes of those kids and helps them to understand that in the same way that those lives are over, their own lives will one day come to an end. He explains to the boys that the kids in those pictures had dreams, too, and yet many of those dreams went unfulfilled.

We have this wonderful gift of life, and each day is its own gift. But distraction can set in, and before we know it, we've missed out on opportunities. We've settled for the easier, more-traveled path. We've traded a risky chance to live extraordinarily for the certainty of living comfortably.

This scares me because I know I've done this. My dream about golfing confirms it.

I've been thinking a lot about vulnerability in an attempt to give myself some courage to pursue wild dreams. There are two stories in the Gospels that seem very similar, and they have been on my mind because of this subject. In Chapter 7 of Luke, a woman who lived a sinful life wet the feet of Christ with her tears, wiped them with her hair, and then poured perfume on them. A Pharisee immediately criticized her in his own mind because of her lifestyle (Luke 7:36-39). In Chapter 12 of John, Mary, the sister of Martha and Lazarus, does a similar thing as she pours expensive perfume on Christ's feet and wipes them with her hair. This time it is one of the disciples that criticizes her, and he does it verbally instead of keeping it to himself (John 12:1-5).

These women have given me some courage. It took extreme vulnerability to do what they did for Christ. Perhaps, they were called to that action; certainly, they were somewhat convicted. And regardless of that conviction or calling, they were still criticized (even by a fellow Christ Follower).

Their actions were unique, too, and spoke of individuality. I don't think men would have been able to repeat their acts of praise. The result was an authentic offering to Christ.

Individuality is another prevalent theme in *Dead Poets Society* because of Mr. Keating's love for Walt Whitman. One of Whitman's main themes in *Leaves of Grass* is individuality, and it seems that this is also required to live extraordinarily:

> That you are here – that life exists and identity,
> That the powerful play goes on, and you may contribute a verse.
> O Me! O Life! (*Leaves of Grass*, 1892)[6]

I like thinking in formulas. I blame my engineering background for that. However, I believe you could take what the women in John's and Luke's Gospels teach us about vulnerability and what Whitman teaches us about individuality, and tie them together in this way:

Individuality + Vulnerability = Authenticity

It is important for me to remember that authentic offerings and actions are still open to criticism. We all experience this. And I think it is wrong for us to just try and dismiss this criticism as if it doesn't bother us. It is criticism of our authentic self, criticism of our core. It will bother us. It will distract and deter us. However, if our actions are done out of authenticity, I think we can at least expect the same response from Christ that He gives the women that John and Luke write about. He accepts their gifts. Cherishes them, in fact. He defends them publicly, even looks past their exterior to their hearts.

He allows us the opportunity to worship Him with our gift in our unique, individual, authentic way. And in doing so, He shares our vulnerability by joining us and making Himself vulnerable, too. He opens Himself up to the exact same criticism that we are exposed to.

Chapter 2

February 2016

The Voice of God Project

2/5/16

    I've been in Fort Myers, Florida for a work trip this week. It is just myself, Kevin, and Matt from the company. We've had such a good time. During the trip, I've tried to maintain the balance described by Paulo Coelho in *The Alchemist*[1]. I have been present with my two work colleagues, whom I also consider to be friends. I have had the urge to be a recluse and to retreat to my room to read, but I have fought it because life is about more than just finishing projects. Life must have community. Besides the work sessions spent with Matt and Kevin, the three of us ran three and a half miles together on a trail around the hotel and kayaked along mangrove islands. But in the evenings and on the plane, I read my February book, *Zen and the Art of Motorcycle Maintenance: An Inquiry into Values*[2], by Robert M. Pirsig.

    This spiritual journey consumes me on a new level now as it's never far from my mind. I had a conversation yesterday with an older lady who was handing out towels at the hotel pool (she actually mentioned in our conversation that she is seventy-five). She was reading *Go Set a Watchman*[3], a book I finished last year. We spoke of disagreement, a strong theme in Harper Lee's book, and how people tend to respond in two ways to those who disagree with them: hate and avoidance. We spoke of the need (more important now than ever before in my life) of listening to one another's hearts rather than just their words, of the need to realize that many times we want to all arrive at the same place, just sometimes by different routes. I am convinced this place is love, joy, peace, patience, kindness, goodness, faithfulness, gentleness, and self-control.

    It became clear to me that Gwyn, my new friend who was distributing towels, will most likely vote differently than me this coming November. That's okay. I did not try to convince her to vote the same way I will, nor did she try to impose her preference on me. I think that is because we have examined each other's hearts and realized that the two of us share the same vision of a country united.

I have really been humbled already this month. Monday, February 1st, I bought some new shoes for my trip. As I was checking out, I overheard two of the store-workers talking. Both were older than me. The whole time I was in the store they had been inventorying their merchandise and recording the numbers on a clipboard. It was about 5:30. The older of the two said, "Well, I'm outta here. I've got to drive to Rivergate and do this again." I, on the other hand, was going home to have dinner with my wife and kids.

On the way home, I told Julie about the conversation. It had really stuck with me. I felt so grateful to have the life I have. I'm not trying to say my life is better than anyone else's, but I feel extremely fortunate (my new favorite word) for my blessings. Having a job that allows me to spend my evenings with my family may not sound like much, but not everyone has that opportunity.

Then I went on this trip to Fort Myers. On Wednesday, Kevin, Matt, and myself went for our run once the day's last session ended. Afterwards, I texted Julie this: "Ran 3.5 miles with Matt and Kevin along a trail here at the resort. Best conference ever. On my tombstone, it needs to say: 'Here lies Brandon. He was a fortunate man.' Kinda can't believe I get to do this with people I really enjoy being around."

The text plays off an inside joke I share with my wife in which I instruct her to use my epitaph as a way to draw pity. The most common example is right after something in the house gets broken (which occurs frequently with little kids): "Here lies Brandon. He couldn't have anything nice."

But the truth is really this: I live a magnificent life. People sarcastically respond to the question "How's it going?" with the phrase "Oh, just living the dream." And people chuckle because everyone knows the truth. This is preposterous. This is absurd. This dream we grew up hearing about is as empty as Allen Iverson's bank account.

But it's different for me because I really am living the dream. Others might scoff at that notion because there is nothing extraordinary about my life, but you won't hear me scoff. You won't hear my wife scoff.

Perhaps, this is the first fruit to be yielded in this spiritual garden. I thought I might see shoots of peace or self-control, but instead, much like C.S. Lewis[4], I find myself surprised by joy (though, unlike him, I don't mean a person).

What a great, overlooked, underrated thing joy is. To be filled with gratitude, thankfulness, and even, to some extent, wonder, is to humble yourself. Then it begins to really hit home how insignificant you are, and the gratitude and feeling of being unworthy consequently deepens. The fruit's seeds scatter and raise more fruit.

This is quite a contrast to how I felt about joy last month. What has changed? Nothing, really. Except my perspective. I'm trying to treasure all these things in my heart.

Now it is my job to weed hard and water and let the fruit grow. I believe joy is a fruit that needs water more than weeding, and I believe the way to do this is by continuing what I've been doing. By capturing the moment at the shoe store and pondering it in my heart, I was able to remind myself how rare it is for people to enjoy the kind of life I enjoy. By capturing the moments at Fort Myers with Matt and Kevin, I was able to ponder it and realize what a special trip it was.

My conclusions are:
1) Capturing a moment is weeding in the Joy Garden.
2) Pondering the moment in my heart is watering the Joy Fruit.
3) Joy is foundational to obtaining love, peace, patience, kindness, goodness, faithfulness, gentleness, and self-control. All of those fruits seem to flow from joy. I am almost convinced it must come first. I mistakenly thought it was conditional, based on the others.

February 2016

2/15/16

So, joy is not as easy as I thought. So many things and people steal it away. Kids can sometimes be as good at stealing joy as they are at giving it. Distractions can be so overwhelming that the resulting stress distorts your view. So much to do and no time to do it in. Or so much bad, you can't dwell on the good.

I got frustrated at home tonight. Something happened, and it seemed like it was the hundredth time. Instead of responding with patience and gentleness, I let my knee-jerk reaction of impatience and harshness kick in. Why do I do that? It doesn't help; it only escalates things and makes things worse. Soon everyone in the house was ill with each other.

Joy = gone.

Then through a series of events, I got frustrated with someone else and a feeling of loneliness enveloped me. I felt like my community had moved on and left me behind, and it was a horrible feeling. Everything just changed so suddenly. One minute, I felt like I was on top of the world and my cup overflowed. The next minute, I felt like people were intentionally trying to hurt me, and my jar felt barren. What a difference a week makes. As I've processed these two events with Julie, we both feel that Satan has a role in this.

Why is it so hard for us to admit that he is active? We sound like kooks, I know. But isn't that part of his plan? Julie has been writing me little notes lately and praying for my writing. She's read my work from last week and loved it. It's all been very encouraging.

So why am I discouraged?

I saw Tony Bartley, my boss from my previous company, today at a meeting. It was so good to talk with him. He sent me a text after we parted that said: "You're like a brother to me." It's a meaningful note, especially considering he has two brothers. It was very encouraging.

So why was I discouraged five minutes later?

The Voice of God Project

2/26/16

Zen and the Art of Motorcycle Maintenance has been a commentary on what Robert M. Pirsig refers to as quality. What is quality? What defines quality? How can something be judged as being of high quality? Pirsig gave examples of reading two essays aloud to his class when he was a professor at a university. Afterwards, he would ask for a show of hands to indicate which of the two essays had better quality. The majority would be in agreement time and again on one essay over another.[5]

But then the difficult question arose: why is that essay better than the other? This was not something the class was able to articulate. If they gave a reason (grammar, language, etc.), he would ask them why they thought those metrics classified one essay to be better than another. In the end, the class could not quantify quality.

The same thoughts could be applied to music or art. Why do some songs become more popular than others? Is it because they have a higher level of quality? Why? Is it the lyrics? Is it the harmonies, the voices? What makes those things good? Why do we prefer those lyrics, harmonies, voices over others?

Taking this a little bit further, why do some people prefer one piece of music while other people prefer a different piece? Why do some people enjoy some styles of art while others do not?

Lately, I've been listening to two movie soundtracks quite a bit (*All is Lost*[6] & *The Cider House Rules*[7]). These are two albums that virtually no one else my age enjoys, at least not on the level I have enjoyed them.

As I've thought about these things, I can't help but be reminded of the scene in *Dead Poets Society* when Mr. Keating makes his students rip out the first part of their textbook that tries to invent a formula to identify good poetry and measure it by a specific set of standards. It can't be done.

And why can't it be done? Because we don't know what quality is. It is not purely subjective, whatever we like. This is obvious by Pirsig's experiments with his students when he compares two separate works. There is always a majority that will commend one work over the other. Something about the work stands out, and everyone knows it. There is something in us that can detect quality, even though we can't put our finger on why we believe something to be high in quality.

Quality also isn't objective. I may see quality in music that others don't like, for instance. Or I may not share an interest in a painting that some other people enjoy. Quality can't be measured. A set of standards cannot be applied to it. It can't be rationalized.

And what in the world does any of this have to do with a spiritual journey centered around the fruit of the Spirit?

Plenty.

You see, the more I've thought about quality, the more I believe that what Robert M. Pirsig refers to as quality is the same thing Paul refers to as goodness. And I think Pirsig's book has helped me to understand goodness in a way I've never thought of it before. In fact, I don't believe anyone has ever taught me explicitly about goodness. It was one of the fruits listed that I always just kind of glossed over. I just associated it with behavior. "Be good." Every parent has given this instruction before. I just thought that when Paul listed this fruit that he was telling us to be good.

But Robert M. Pirsig has helped me to understand goodness on a newer, deeper level.

Goodness, like quality, isn't subjective, art, hedonistic. Goodness isn't objective, science, logical.

Goodness is spirituality, God, a part of our design left by our Creator.

When God spoke the world into existence in Genesis, He saw that it was good (Genesis 1:4, 10, 12, 18, 21, 25, 31). But I don't think He was simply observing goodness or giving His opinion of His own work. He was *declaring* His work good. This is the origin of goodness. It comes from Him. He created it, thus He determined what it is that is good. Goodness is as complex as the one who made it.

By speaking the world into creation, God spoke an element of Himself into creation. Since then, even the derivations of the words good and god have a closely-related history. In fact, the word enthusiasm means to be filled with *theos*, filled with God. Goodness is *God's*-ness.

So, goodness happens when a piece of the creator's soul is put into his or her work. Appreciating goodness is the language of souls: when our souls connect with the souls of creators. It's our soul recognizing God in His world, in His work. It is when the soul of a musician speaks to the souls of his audience, or when the soul of an artist speaks to the soul of someone who admires her painting. We don't understand the language of souls, but our soul interprets it for us. It is the portion of God that He gave us when He declared us *very good*. Then, without knowing why, we can take a book, a song, a photo, a painting, a sculpture, a poem, a relationship, a touch and call it good.

Understanding goodness is a pre-requisite to recognizing it, and I think that is what *Zen and the Art of Motorcycle Maintenance* has done for me. Being aware of and recognizing goodness in people is like recognizing that part of us still left intact after the fall, that part of us that is like God. And doing things that are good doesn't mean having acceptable behavior; it means reflecting God in our life's actions. Just the other day, Wilson preached on the Good Samaritan, and I couldn't help thinking that also means the God-like Samaritan, which deepens the meaning of the story even more. This person's behavior wasn't just good; it was the way God Himself would behave in that situation. Then I can see the story as not only a way I should act (me in the Samaritan's place), but also as a way that God interacts with me (me in the traveler's place).

In other words, I believe the story of the Good Samaritan in Luke 10:25-37 also teaches me about God. Compare how the Good Samaritan responds to crisis with how God responds. The Good Samaritan did not prevent the assault, but he did take pity on the man. He treated the man's wounds. He let the man use his own donkey to get him to an inn where the man would find help. He provides for the man's care and makes sure the man is surrounded by people who will help him.

Perhaps this parable is not only a way to instruct us on how to be a good neighbor. Perhaps this parable also teaches us how God responds to moments in our lives where we are met with tragedy. Perhaps this parable teaches us not only about the goodness of the Samaritan but also the goodness of God.

We see an example of how people work in good ways to contribute to the overall goodness of God's will. And then we can look at both the goodness of the big picture, as well as the goodness of each subsystem. Goodness in everything; the goodness of each part, each mechanical inventory, the reverence for the function of each part, the reverence for the entire system.

A life can be worse than one that is filled with a constantly discerning quest for goodness. For a true, heart-driven pursuit of goodness is nothing short of a pursuit of God Himself.

And so, when I read a book and consider it good, I believe that it is the author's goodness connecting to my goodness on a soul-to-soul level. When I create, write, work, play, speak, befriend, it is my goodness connecting with those recipients of these actions. It is my soul connecting with the souls of others.

Vulnerability, then, is the baring of our souls so that those connections can occur.

One of the reasons it has taken me so long to finish reading Pirsig's book is because I have spent so much of my time writing my own book about a carpenter, trying to do the one thing that I can never be sure of: make it good. Hours and hours have been spent in order to produce about 15,000 words. Whether anyone else will consider it good, I don't know.

But it contains a part of me. A deep, vulnerable part. My soul, my goodness.

Chapter 3

March 2016

The Voice of God Project

3/11/16

I can tell this month is going to be powerful. I've gone back to nonfiction with *One Thousand Gifts: A Dare to Live Fully Right Where You Are* by Ann Voskamp[1]. Partly because I feel it will greatly complement *Zen and the Art of Motorcycle Maintenance* and the focus of recognizing goodness and living in the present. I'm about a quarter of the way through the book, and I have fallen in love with Voskamp's poetic writing style.

3/16/16

A few guys and myself have been reading together through a book called *The Way of the Heart: Connecting with God through Prayer, Wisdom, and Silence* by Henri Nouwen[2]. Recently, our guys' group finished our study of the book. The last section was about prayer. Nouwen talked about prayer much in the same way I've recently talked about goodness. He also talked extensively about how there is no understanding in prayer, and it triggered a thought. (It's funny how staying focused on two verses for a year can impact your understanding of them. My mind is never far from the fruit of the Spirit.)

When Nouwen made his comment about no understanding in prayer, I realized (for the first time) that there is also no understanding in the Spirit. Understanding is not a fruit. Paul tells us of all the things we can expect from the Spirit; understanding is not one of them.

I taught an adult Bible class this past Wednesday evening, and the topic of the class was "Does the Holy Spirit transform us?"

I was struggling with the topic of the class. I had to ask myself what I really believed. I mean, I want to believe that the Holy Spirit transforms us, but there is a big part of me that feels like people are just who they are and they don't change. I've known several people that have longed for transformation, but they just can't seem to beat their addiction or get over their own selfishness.

In *Holy Spirit, Here and Now*, Trevor Hudson suggests we think of the

Holy Spirit not as an "it" but as a person.[3] Well, that got me thinking about the people in the Bible that were transformed by meeting Christ. I thought that by their examples I could help define transformation, which would help me to compare their experiences with my own. Of course, there are those who are healed by a physical illness or disability, and they are transformed immediately. This is how I've always viewed transformation, and studying those experiences did nothing to help convince me that in today's world one can be transformed by the Holy Spirit.

But then I came across Nicodemus. In the third chapter of John, Nicodemus comes to Jesus very privately at night. His first words are to tell Jesus that he knows He is a teacher who has come from God (John 3:2). I'm convinced that he starts here simply because he doesn't know where else to start. I'm not even certain Nicodemus knows why he is visiting Christ. Usually, when you go see someone (especially privately, like under the cover of night), you have something specific to ask that person. But Nicodemus doesn't know what he is even asking for. So, he just starts with what he knows and lets Christ direct the conversation.

And Christ has no problem with meeting Nicodemus where he is and then moving the conversation along. He immediately responds to this confession of Nicodemus by telling him that he needs to be born again if he wants to see the kingdom of God (John 3:3). Christ knows more about the reason Nicodemus is visiting Him than Nicodemus himself.

Nicodemus must be thinking Christ is joking with him because he makes this silly reply about entering his mother's womb (John 3:4). His sarcastic tone indicates that he himself is joking back at the teacher, almost as if he's saying, "That's a good one Jesus. I'll stop by my mother's house on the way home, and if she's not busy, I'll climb back into her womb." But Jesus once again takes command of the conversational tone as He tells Nicodemus He is serious. He then gives a brief and complex explanation of how the Spirit works (John 3:5-8).

It is when Nicodemus replies the second time that he admits he doesn't understand.

"How can this be?" Nicodemus asked (John 3:9).

I can almost hear his thinking: "I am a scholar. No one knows more about this than me. So, why am I so confused?"

Nicodemus enters Christ's presence as a Pharisee and leaves Christ's presence as a Pharisee. By all appearances, he seems unchanged by his interaction with Christ. I think that if you asked Nicodemus immediately afterward, even he would deny any transformation from his meeting with the Teacher. In fact, a few chapters later in John 7 we see a reemergence of Nicodemus, and this time he is having a conversation with his fellow Pharisees. The Pharisees are all worked up and ready to condemn Christ, but Nicodemus offers a voice of reason:

"Does our law condemn a man without hearing him to find out what he has been doing?" (John 7:51).

In other words, "Fellas, slow down. Remember our law. Let's just hear him out. Sheesh, you guys have changed."

But the Pharisees don't respond well to Nicodemus:

They replied, "Are you from Galilee, too?" (John 7:52).

In other words, "No, Nicodemus. You are the one who has changed."

It is ironic that the Pharisees (remember the Bible indicates *they* replied, so it wasn't just one of them) ask him if he is from Galilee because in a way that remark alludes to his origin, which alludes to his birth and somewhat plays on Christ's words of being born again. I wonder if this irony struck Nicodemus in that moment, though I'm almost positive he found himself looking around at his fellow Pharisees, his holy brothers, and wondering when they became so different from him. Or did it occur to him that it was actually he that was becoming different from them?

Finally, Nicodemus is seen one more time in John's gospel in Chapter

19. He, along with Joseph of Arimathea, are the two people that prepare the body of Christ for burial (John 19:38-42). Nicodemus brings with him seventy-five pounds of a perfumed ointment, the amount appropriate for a king's burial. Nicodemus no longer thinks of Christ as just a teacher. He is ready to anoint Him King.

It was the example of Nicodemus that helped me to recognize what transformation looks like. It's gradual. Sometimes others see it in you before you see it in yourself. I actually think that Jesus recognized transformation in Nicodemus during their conversation in John 3. I think that is why Jesus directed the conversation toward the topic of transformation, or being born again. He saw that the heart of Nicodemus was already undergoing some transformation, and in John 7, the Pharisees recognized it, too.

This example also shows that transformation can happen before you understand everything. Understanding is not a prerequisite. In fact, as we mentioned, understanding is not even listed as a fruit of the Spirit. We don't have to know it all. I'm convinced that Nicodemus didn't even know where to start. He began his conversation with Jesus by acknowledging that Jesus was from God, but this was just an introductory statement. He didn't know where to go from there. But Jesus did.

I also think it is interesting that this whole transformation began with a private meeting with Jesus. I've always wanted to give Nicodemus a hard time about his secret meeting with Jesus at night. There's a part of me that first read that interaction between Jesus and Nicodemus and thought that Jesus was a little bit rude to the Pharisee, maybe due to the secrecy of the meeting. But I was wrong. Christ wasn't being rude; He was helping Nicodemus focus on what was important. The privacy and secrecy of the meeting didn't prevent Jesus from helping the Pharisee.

Transformation defined in this structure is transformation I can believe in. It is precisely this un-extraordinary way that my own life has been and is being transformed.

3/24/16

One Thousand Gifts talks extensively of transformation. It also comments strongly on two spiritual fruits: 1) Joy and 2) Goodness. Ann Voskamp ties joy to giving thanks, and giving thanks comes from recognizing God's gifts, His goodness in the world.

Throughout the book, she is compiling a list of things for which she is thankful. But this is unlike any gratitude list I have ever seen. She wants to be very specific, which requires a new level of awareness for her to identify one thousand different things in her life that reflect God's goodness. This takes intentionality, and she compares the approach required to none other than the work required to grow fruit in garden beds.

She develops an appreciation for everything around her that is unique as she treasures God's constant gifts. By being specific about the items she records on her list, she experiences thankfulness on a deeper level. The ability to be aware of and recognize goodness, according to Ann Voskamp, leads directly to joy. So, by intentionally looking for God's goodness and recording it in her journal, she experiences joy on a new level.

"The gift list *is* thinking upon His goodness."[4]

This book also gave me a good reminder of what I'm trying to achieve from this modern spiritual journey.

> "I can't leave crowd for mountaintop, daily blur for Walden Pond – but there's always the possibility of singular vision. I remember: Contemplative simplicity isn't a matter of circumstances; it's a matter of *focus*."[5]

This is exactly what I'm trying to do with this year of spiritual journey. To still be husband, father, friend, worker and also to plant seeds that I know will grow fruit and to weed the garden so that the fruit can grow.

Once again, I am reminded of the two times that Luke records Mary treasuring up things in her heart (Luke 2:19, 51). *One Thousand Gifts* seems to be a practical guide for how to mimic this behavior of Mary's. Though still intimidating, I at least feel hopeful that it is achievable.

3/28/16

Yesterday, Easter Sunday, the Sullivans were both baptized. We left our GPS room as a class and walked to the auditorium. All the lights were off, except for one at the baptistry. While Jason, Janna, and Wilson were getting ready, Van led us in song. Heather asked if I would like to hold Baby Henry, and he snuggled right into the crook of my elbow. I was at the back of the crowd and on a lower step. As I looked forward, I could not directly see the baptistry nor the light. But I could see all the faces around me. Two sweet ladies, each pregnant and eager to meet their first child. Faces young, faces old, each singing the same song. Mothers and fathers holding newborns and singing from the mountaintop. Others hurting and singing from the pit. Each face was different, but each face was reflecting the light, the same light, the very light that husband and wife are baptized into. Each smiling face shone the light in their own unique way, but they were all, different though they were, united by the light. And husband, wife, father, mother emerged from the waters and carried the light with them.

4/2/16

I am sitting and watching friends throw a Frisbee at retreat. Dusty, Heather, and Baby Henry pass by, and mother instructs child to tell me, "hello". John and Amy pass by next, and I'm always captivated by this couple and their ability to commune quietly. I see Hannah, who welcomed me with a hug. She is showing, her son's presence becoming evident, and I think back to two years ago when David informed us of the existence of Lyndon here at this very retreat. A couple (I can't see who) is stretched out on a towel in the sun while the group puts the disc up and trades it for a bocce ball.

I listen as wind announces God's presence, and I think of goodness in terms of what I've learned from Robert Pirsig and Ann Voskamp. Goodness – our soul glimpsing original design, heavenly intention.

I love all of these people. David just made a great shot, and everyone cheers with him. Then I think of how everyone has hoped with him, grieved with him. As I watch another friend, Daniel, I think of how last year he was so miserable in his job and was getting calls about a new job during the retreat. I think of how he got the job offer and how he turned it down. We all prayed for him, discerned with him as he made a difficult decision.

One final note on joy: today Caleb played his first soccer game. Fay got a picture of him running with a wide smile on his face. He didn't do anything special. I think he only kicked the ball once (and barely). But he had joy. And as I watched that, then went to retreat, it hit me that his joy came from being a part of something, being a part of a team. And I get joy from being a part of this community. He found joy from running with his team, chasing a ball, and I find joy from journeying with this group, chasing God. The joy is not in kicking the ball as much as pursuing it with people you love.

Chapter 4

April 2016

The Voice of God Project

4/18/16

I'm a mess. I feel like I've taken a giant step backwards in this journey this month. I feel overrun by despair to the point that sometimes things seem hopeless. And I've done a pathetic job of journaling about it. It's funny how quickly your spiritual garden can be overcome by weeds when you aren't diligent about the weeding.

I am reading, though. I'm more than three hundred pages into *The Cider House Rules*[1] by John Irving, which is my April book. But the weeds are out of control, which has kept me from getting much out of this book so far except that it's a good story. The weeds are so thick, to the point that I don't know where to start.

I'm not processing things well, which was the whole point of *One Thousand Gifts*. What's the point of this experiment if I'm not going to allow what I've learned to change how I live? Instead of capturing each moment and pondering it in my heart and thereby hearing the voice of God, I've allowed myself to become distracted by all the other voices of the world. Sometimes I just can't shut them out. My mind never stops, and it can make life hard to enjoy.

It's ironic. Wrestling with the things going on in my life (and not even just in my life, but in the world in general) is precisely what I should be doing, but this worrying about it all the time is a distracted form of wrestling. What I really need to do is process it all, make some sort of sense of it all. I'm not even sure how I feel about some of it; I need to sort my feelings out. It's all so overwhelming.

So, let me be specific and see if I can explain any of this to myself. Let me try to put into words the complex language of my soul. Let me take a moment to look for God's goodness by removing the weeds that are trying to choke it out. After all, there are plenty of good things going on.

First off, Julie is expecting. We're going to be having our third child some time in November. This is fantastic. The two of us spent a lot of time talking last year about growing our family. I like the idea of having a big family, doing life together, spending important moments of our lives with each other. I think that when I'm hopefully old and at the end of my life, I will look back at my personal accomplishments, and they will pale in comparison to my children. I can't help but think of future Thanksgivings and Christmases with a house full of kids and grandkids.

I'm also thrilled about having a baby in the house once more. The whole baby thing seems new again. It has been four years since we last expected a baby. I get to make another nursery for my child, an opportunity I never thought I'd have again. That was a sweet and sacred event for me when I worked on rooms for Caleb and Lucy as I awaited them. It reminds of Christ saying that He's going to prepare a place for us (John 14:2-3). I love having the opportunity to do exactly that for my children.

But I'm scared, too. This has kind of caught me off guard. I was the main one who first expressed the desire of having another baby. It can be scary to think about bringing a child into this crazy world, but I couldn't ignore this desire to do exactly that. I just think we have this great love for each other, and I want to invite another life to be a part of that.

When God mentioned that it was not good for man to be alone, I can apply what I've learned about goodness and realize that Genesis 2:18 can be translated as, "It is not God-like for man to be alone." In other words, I believe God desires community (He *is* a community of three beings in one, after all). And when I think about God's reasoning for creating mankind, I believe it is for the same reason that I want to have another child. God is love, and that love is so strong that He wants to share it with others. And even though it is going to be crazy and messy, that overwhelming love drives us (and God) to be willing to enter into that crazy mess in order to establish a relationship of love.

I'm not sure what Caleb and Lucy are going to think about having a baby around, though. They are going to have to share a bedroom. With them being six and four, hopefully that won't be a big issue, but everything is going to be harder. Of course, I knew that, but it seems like those words hold more gravity for me now.

I feel like I'm closer with Caleb and Lucy than ever before. What will bringing another child into the house do to that? We've been very intentional about spending time together lately because Caleb will be going to Kindergarten this Fall. That is hitting me kind of hard. We won't be able to do things together on my Fridays off anymore. Where did that phase of our lives go? How can he already be this old?

I'm worried about him going to Kindergarten. Will he have friends? Will his teacher like him? Is school going to be hard for him? He's got the sweetest little heart in the world. He's always doing for others, always concerned for others. Will he keep that? Will it be stolen away? These are the thoughts that dominate my thinking.

Other good things are going on, too. I've been asked to submit an abstract to a national engineering conference on some engineering work I did a couple of years ago. It's still a long shot that my abstract will be selected as they have a large amount of submissions. Just getting this opportunity means a lot to me, though.

I told my father-in-law, John, about it the other day in a very nonchalant manner, as if it wasn't a very big deal. Of course, I was excited, but I played it down like I was just chit-chatting about the events of my week. After all, my abstract may not be selected. In fact, I wasn't even going to tell him about it at all but decided to bring it up as we were getting ready to leave.

But after I finished telling him about it, I turned to get into the car and he grabbed my shoulder kind of firmly. He turned me back around to face him, looked directly into my eyes and said, "I'm so proud of you." That was it. Then he turned to go into his house, and I climbed into the car. But I got pretty emotional after he left. Even now, my eyes are moist as I recall the story.

The reason for this emotion is because of how rocky things started for me when I first started this job. I really didn't think I was going to make it. I felt so out of place, like I was in over my head. All of my training was in another field of engineering, and I was starting over. It was miserable. And now, I've been asked to present at a national conference on a project I did. Most engineers would kill for an opportunity like this, and I'm not technically even doing engineering work anymore. Life is mysterious.

I even sent my first query letter on the book I've been working on, and the agent replied the same day asking to see my manuscript. This doesn't mean much other than I did a good job on the query letter. Who knows if I'll actually hear back from him, but at least he's willing to look at the book. I really didn't expect to get that far.

In all of this, I can't help but think about Julie and at the same time feel somewhat guilty. I have a career I enjoy, and she is doing the kids' laundry. I received an email about being in a young professional program the other day, but one of the qualifications was that applicants had to be under thirty-five years old. It hit me that I'm almost too old to be considered a young professional. Julie never even got the chance. Thinking of her more has helped me to think about myself less. She certainly has thought about herself less these past six years. It hasn't been easy for her to put her career on hold for so long, but she is doing what she feels like is best for our family. Her example of selflessness has affected people throughout her entire life.

Perhaps, in fruit terms, kindness is thinking about yourself less.

There are a lot of good things going on in my world, and just writing them down and listing them with some detail (a lesson I've learned from Ann Voskamp) has made me realize yet again how fortunate I am.

The Voice of God Project

But life is not so simple. In fact, despite these amazing events, I feel more longing than I feel joy. My mind is constantly going. It has been that way for me since I was a little kid. In fact, it used to keep me up night after night. The big questions, the hard questions. Yes, my personal world is going well, but my thoughts are constantly dominated by what's going on in the larger world. My heart longs for a world put to rights. My soul aches for justice and peace. The sense of calling that goes along with that consumes me.

Let me be more specific. The reality that we live in a broken world is more evident than ever before in my lifetime. With the events of the Brussels tragedy still so fresh, it seems like the whole world is divided. There is a prevalence of dissension and even hatred. Violence seems widespread. It is easier for people to find things to disagree on than things to agree on.

How can you raise children in this world? How will they find good friends? A spouse that will love them? A community that supports them? When the world turns its back on peace, contentment, and selflessness, how does your child have any alternative but to do likewise?

These questions haunt me. I struggle to relinquish control. I see injustice, and it eats at me. I see division among each cultural group: race against race, faith against faith against faithless, sexual orientation against sexual orientation, income class against income class, the battle between citizens and police and politicians.

I witness these things, and I hurt for the world. I want to put the world to rights. I know deep down that I can't, and yet I cannot escape the feeling that it is my calling. I remember a person asked me once how I thought I could fix the world's problems when Christ Himself could not. I have no answers. And yet, still it eats at me.

I am struggling with how to be filled with the Spirit when the world is empty of it. I'm struggling to not allow myself to get sucked into a whirlpool of hopelessness.

There is a song called *Vita Nostra*[2] by Ennio Morricone that is part of *The Mission* soundtrack. When the song starts, it is mainly an oboe with a subtle drum playing behind it. However, as the song progresses, there are some strings added, voices singing in Latin, and even the sound of maracas creeps in. And pretty soon, the background sounds get louder and faster until they take over the music played by the oboe.

I feel like life is this way. The voice of God is so clear, just like the oboe. But slowly and subtly, the noise of the world comes along and drowns God out. Yes, it's still there, still playing its melody. No, it hasn't gotten any quieter. It's just harder to hear because it's battling with all the other noises of the world.

Never before in my life has it been so hard for me to listen for the true voice of God.

4/24/16

Well, if I thought I was undergoing any sort of transformation during this spiritual journey, I can safely dismiss that notion right now. I did something I'm not proud of yesterday. I can't believe how bad I am at displaying the fruit of the Spirit in my own life. I'm not someone who is thought of as loving, joyful, peaceful, patient, kind, good, gentle, faithful, and certainly not self-controlling. I am someone who is frustrated, anxious, and impatient.

I yelled at a volunteering parent at Caleb's soccer game yesterday. While I didn't like the way he was talking to my son, that's no excuse. The parent raised his voice at Caleb a few times, and I was able to let some of it go. But it was a real struggle for me. Julie must have known how hard it was for me because she wrapped her arm around mine one time and whispered to me, "It's okay, Brandon."

I made it nearly through the entire game, but then near the end of the third quarter something happened, and before I even realized it, I was standing up shouting across the field, "Will you just let them play?!?"

I immediately regretted it. He got mad, took his kid, and left. I tried to apologize, but he didn't want to hear it. I can't say I blame him. I probably embarrassed him. I certainly embarrassed myself. Especially when my good friends Bob and Blair (who help run the soccer program, who I go to church with – where I'm a deacon!) came over to me and said, "We heard there was someone over here causing a scene."

It was humiliating for me to admit, "Um...that would be me." The guy who wants to put the world to rights.

I felt sick to my stomach. I was mad at myself. I was mad at the guy who yelled at my son. I was mad at everyone who witnessed me losing my self-control. I was mad in general at this whole fallen world and how easy it is to fall into discord instead of peace.

And you know what else? I was mad at the Spirit. After all, I'm doing this whole journey to sow seeds to grow this fruit. Where is it? Why isn't it present? Why is my first reaction still to act in complete opposite ways of the Spirit? I want these behaviors to be ingrained in me; I want them to be a part of who I am, part of my DNA.

I thought the whole world was hopeless. Was I that wrong? Was it me all along who was truly hopeless?

I wonder if Paul felt this way. In 2 Corinthians 12:7-9, Paul talks about a thorn in his flesh that keeps him from being conceited. No one knows what this thorn is, but there is a lot of speculation. Most of the time it centers around something physical, like Paul's eyesight. Perhaps his eyesight was bad. Or maybe it was that he never got married. Bible experts have their theories.

And me, not being a Bible expert, should probably refrain from a theory, but I cannot help thinking that this thorn has less to do with his physical condition and marital status as it has to do with his baggage, his reputation, his shame.

April 2016

Paul persecuted Christians. He witnessed and approved the stoning of Stephen. He went door to door and put people in prison because of their faith (Acts 8-9). Now, this is just me completely speculating, but I have to be pretty naïve to think that people didn't bring this up to Paul as he was trying to spread God's word.

I wonder how he felt when people reminded him of who he used to be. I wonder if he ever ran into the children he turned into orphans when he imprisoned their parents.

I don't know. Again, I'm just speculating.

But if this did happen, I can understand why he would pray to God to take that shame and that reputation away. I know I've done stupid things that I wish could be taken away.

But if nothing else, I should feel comfort in God's response to him:

"My grace is sufficient for you…" (2 Cor. 12:9)

In other words, "You may never shake your reputation. Some people may never let you live down your misdeeds. You may always be seen as the person who behaved that certain way. The world may never forgive you. But I do. And that's enough."

This is the message I must remember as I try hard to go about making my character more closely align with the character of my Maker.

Because I will mess up.

And I will be reminded of what I've done.

And I will have to live with that.

But that's okay. Because God's grace is sufficient for me.

5/5/16

I finished *The Cider House Rules* by John Irving on Friday, April 29th. The novel is a story of Dr. Wilbur Larch, who runs an orphanage that also serves as a hospital. One of the boys that grows up in that orphanage is Homer Wells, whom Dr. Larch loves as if Homer was his own son. However, they begin to disagree on the direction Homer's life should take as he grows up. Dr. Larch thinks Homer should carry on the work that Dr. Larch himself has been doing, but Homer meets a girl and gets the desire to see another part of the world. There is also some disagreement on the way Dr. Larch carries out his practice that Homer has to make up his own mind about.

While I didn't agree with everything in it, I did enjoy Irving's novel. It was a fun read, but it also had some sweet moments. I think that I was sort of struggling for a while with whether or not a fruit might exist in this book. After all, there are some morally compromising themes throughout. I kept looking to Homer to provide this fruit, but instead, it was an unlikely character who came through.

Dr. Larch may be abrasive on the exterior, but deep down, he has a servant heart. In fact, I created a term that I think helps describe the way he approached life and treated people: compassionate irritation. Now, that sounds harsh, but I honestly mean it as a compliment. Dr. Larch may come off as bitter, uncaring, and superior because of his personality, but in reality, his mission in life is to be "of use." This is a term he frequently uses and a way of life he instructs the orphans to put into practice.

He loves people, but he is also absolutely frustrated by them. He is not comfortable being around people; the way they behave and the trouble they cause (sometimes to themselves) makes no sense to Dr. Larch. In other words, he doesn't appear to me to be at home in this world. I think he is as irritated with the way this world works as I am. And yet, he doesn't let that prevent him from helping the world. He may not love people with his words, but he does so with his actions.

Compassionate irritation – a desire to serve the world in which one finds oneself, even though one finds oneself at complete odds with the world.

I certainly may not agree with some of Dr. Larch's methods of serving, but as misguided as I believe they are, his intention is still to serve those around him. Even though I may disagree with Dr. Larch, I still believe there is something to be learned by his attitude toward helping others.

The fruit that has stuck out to me from this book has been kindness. I defined kindness earlier as thinking about yourself less (not less of yourself). I have heard people define humility in this way, and I wonder if kindness and humility aren't the same thing. John 3:30 – "He must increase, but I must decrease" – appears to me to be the root of kindness. How much humbler an attitude can one have?

The reason kindness sticks out to me is because of Dr. Larch's life mission to be "of use." While Dr. Larch's interpretation of being of use included some politically and morally complex positions, I think having a mindset to be "of use" to the world is a good approach to serving.

This reminds me of another quote that spoke to me from *Awakenings*. It happens when Dr. Sayer is watching a video of Leonard's progress. At this point of the film, Leonard has completely relapsed into the catatonic state he was in when Dr. Sayer first met him. As he's watching the video, Nurse Costello walks into the room. Dr. Sayer asks her about something that has been on his mind.

> Dr. Sayer: You told him I was a kind man. How kind is it to give life, only to take it away again?
> Nurse Costello: It's given and taken away from all of us.
> Dr. Sayer: Why doesn't that comfort me?
> Nurse Costello: Because you are a kind man.[3]

In other words, kindness (as well as the other fruits of the Spirit) does not spare us hurt. No, the opposite is actually true. The curse of the fruit of the Spirit is that those who take it on also take on the burden of those in and around their own lives.

So, what does this tell me about God?

If kindness is a fruit of God's Spirit, then it is part of His nature. Sometimes it is easy to think of God as someone who is detached and indifferent about the world He created. But this cannot be the case. God, because of His nature of being kind, is also deeply compassionate to the point where He cannot be indifferent. Like Dr. Sayer, His kindness prevents Him from rationalizing situations to comfort Himself. He is not immune to hurting. He takes on our burdens. Because of His nature, He suffers with those of us who are suffering.

Thinking about kindness, particularly God's kindness, reminds me of a middle school boys Bible class I led on Wednesday nights years ago. We were talking about some pretty heavy stuff, and sometimes the questions got so deep that I couldn't sufficiently answer them.

I remember one night there was a boy that raised his hand and said he had a question. But instead of asking a question, he started talking about this kid in his class at school and how this kid was really a nice guy but he didn't believe in God. This obviously weighed heavily on the boy's mind, and after rambling for a few minutes, he just sort of stopped talking. He never actually asked a question.

So, I asked him, "And what's your question?"

He looked lost. He said, "I guess, I don't know. I just…I just wish everyone could go to Heaven."

What do you say to that? The room was silent, waiting for an answer. It was obvious that this boy's sentiment for the world to be saved was shared by every other boy in that Wednesday night Bible class. I felt the same exact way. And yet, I had no answer.

It was several days later when I realized that God also wants everyone to go to Heaven. After all, that is why He went through the pain of sending Christ. That compassion for others that all of us in that room shared with God – that is kindness.

Chapter 5

May and June 2016

The Voice of God Project

5/13/16

In Matthew 5:9, Jesus says, "Blessed are the peacemakers." This verse comes to mind when I think of *The Brothers Karamazov*[1] by Fyodor Dostoevsky, my book for the month of May (and likely June, due to its length). The two characters I have fallen in love with are Father Zosima, an elder at the monastery who is well-loved by the people, and Alyosha, his disciple. These two have taken to task the life of selflessness. And one who is dedicated to selflessness, in principle, is a peacemaker.

This brings to mind the statement Paul makes in Philippians 4:7 when he writes that the peace of God transcends all understanding. The King James Version translates this to say that the peace of God *passes* understanding. I looked up the original Greek word used for the verb transcend or pass, and it means to be of more value than something.

I think I have misunderstood this verse for a long time. I don't know that transcend is the best word for this context. The English Standard Version translates this word as "surpass," and I think this is more appropriate to the original Greek definition.

Why does this matter? Because for so long I thought that the peace of God was going to transcend me and my understanding. In other words, I had this picture of a person who lived a completely peaceful life, a *transcendent* life. Now, however, I don't think that is what Paul meant at all. I think he simply meant that peace is more important than understanding.

What does this have to do with being a peacemaker? A peacemaker not only doesn't care who is right or wrong, he or she sacrifices all validation of his or her own opinion for the prize of peace. It is more important to a peacemaker for peace to exist than it is to be right.

The opposite of this attitude can be seen in the character of Grigory, a man who cares more about being right and convincing others to believe as he does than he cares about others themselves. Anyone who disagrees with him instantly becomes his enemy. It is my observation that the world is full of Grigorys (those who sincerely believe they are living as children of God should) and rare is the occasional Alyosha found.

5/20/16

I have a friend that is a peacemaker. In fact, I witnessed that firsthand recently. The two of us have been at odds with each other for a little while. Silly things have crept in and put a wedge between us. Without going into much detail, some things happened that bothered me, and I never told my friend about them. He was completely unaware, which, for some reason, bothered me more.

Instead of processing any of it or dealing with it, I just got to where I avoided him. Then one day when we were talking, it just came out. Of course, since I had let it build up over time, it did not come out very diplomatically. And just as I was feeling very Grigory-ish, my friend reminded me how similar he is to Alyosha.

He asked if we could get together and talk, and when we did, he just listened as I vented. Afterwards, he explained some of what happened and apologized for any misunderstanding. I felt like I was the one who should apologize. Why had I let things get to such a point? I had let things stew so much that I had become convinced that I was right.

And worst of all, I went into my meeting with my friend with the goal to show him I was right. My friend, on the other hand, came into the meeting with the goal of making peace.

Afterward, I was thinking about the fruit of the Spirit again and how they apply to our meeting. Obviously, love and peace are prevalent fruits that I had just experienced. My friend was willing to go into an uncomfortable environment and have a difficult discussion, all in the name of making peace. You have to really love someone if you are going to make yourself available to hear difficult things about yourself from him or her. Having a discussion like this is extremely awkward. You become particularly vulnerable when you enter into this kind of environment.

The Voice of God Project

And that leads me to another fruit that has come to mind – a fruit that I've often wondered why it was included in the list with the other eight. Gentleness.

I have wondered what gentleness is since the beginning of this journey, particularly in relation to the fruit of the Spirit. I tell my kids all the time to be gentle. I try to teach them to be gentle as a way to prevent their things from breaking. Because once a toy is broken, it sometimes can't be fixed, and the damage is then permanent.

Maybe gentleness, as it is referred to as a fruit of the Spirit, is simply treating the vulnerability of others with the delicacy it deserves. A person's vulnerability is their most fragile component. Treating it roughly will leave the person damaged, perhaps sometimes in a way that cannot be repaired. But being gentle ensures the person will remain whole, complete, and preserved for the future.

In a world where it is more common to treat people harshly (especially people in conflict with you), I'm thankful to have a friend who practices gentleness.

6/15/16

Three days ago, there was a terrible tragedy that happened in Orlando, Florida. Fifty people were killed senselessly, probably targeted because of their lifestyle. The Orlando incident is heartbreaking on so many levels. How can a person have so much evil inside of them? How can so much hate for other human beings exist?

I am so disappointed in the response of our nation and its leaders. *Ban guns! Ban immigrants!* Perhaps some policies need investigation and modification, but I am tired of treating the symptoms rather than the disease.

There is hate in this country and in this world. I believe it roots itself in the thought that "they are different than me", but stems itself into "they want me to be like them" and "they don't respect me" and "they think they're better than me." And we seem to let the way we respond further divide us.

Franklin Roosevelt's quote that "the only thing to fear is fear itself" is so true and so relevant today. I'm not sure I ever understood what he was saying, but these words are finally developing some meaning for me. When our decisions and behaviors are driven by fear, we let that emotion have too much control, and we end up doing stupid and hurtful things. We respond to hate with hate and divisiveness with divisiveness. Our nation should be grieving together, not picking fights with each other over our different agendas.

I believe this whole slacktivism idea is a behavior subconsciously rooted in fear. I know that sounds crazy, but I think deep down that putting a flag filter over a profile picture, signing an online petition, or even tweeting out a prayer hashtag is nothing more than an attempt to control the situation. I mean, who needs to know that we're praying, other than God? Why are we making it a point to tell everyone else? I mean, would Daniel have tweeted out that he was going to pray, regardless of Darius's new decree? #stillgonnapraythreetimesaday

It's admirable that we want to make the world a better place, but it's naïve to think we can do that simply with a hashtag or online post. We're not that powerful. We're not that influential.

You know what I love the most about Father Zosima? He constantly reflects God. When people come to him for help, he doesn't tell those people what he is doing or what he will do or even what they should do. He reminds them of who God is, and tells them what God is doing.

I think this tragedy should be met with what God's doing, not what we're doing. That is how Father Zosima would respond. This is when people need to be reminded the most of the character of God. I wish these celebrities that are posting "Prayers for Orlando" would post something more like: "The reason I can have hope in these moments is because I know that God is mourning along with us, that He's a God who loves and is hurt by the hate prevalent among His children. He lost fifty of His children tonight, His masterpieces, souls whose bodies He formed in their mothers' wombs. As difficult as it is to understand the evil that took place and as scary as it is to live in this world sometimes, I can have hope because of a good God who grieves alongside our grieving nation."

But that is more than 140 characters, so…how about a hashtag?

Bottom line: we should tell what God is doing, not what we are doing. Oh, I know it is important to pray for the victims and families of the victims. And what a sweet sentiment to share with others that you are praying. But this sentiment is met with skepticism and cynicism for unbelievers or people who have an image of God as a being who loves to punish instead of just loves.

That is why it is important for us to remind people what God is like. Jesus told His disciples in Acts 1:8 to be His witnesses. We don't have to be Christ, just Christ's witness. That is a lot less intimidating to me. I can't be Christ, but I can be a witness. After all, what does a witness do? He or she simply relays information. It's not the role of the witness in a trial to put a person in jail or get a person's charges dropped. Witnesses say what they've seen. Witnesses show what they know. Christ's witnesses should follow these same guidelines. They don't tell what they have done; they tell what God has done. They remind people who God is. They teach people God's nature.

This was the whole point behind Christ's teachings. He clearly represented God's nature when He told parables, answered questions, and taught the crowds. I've heard it said that Jesus was a radical, but I respectfully disagree. His teachings seemed rather radical because they were different than what the people were used to; they weren't what the people were expecting.

But I don't think that makes Jesus a radical. In fact, it only goes to show how confused people were about God's nature. God hadn't changed in the time between the Garden of Eden and the Garden of Gethsemane. People just didn't understand. Christ's teachings were to correct all the misunderstandings, not change up or eradicate any previous teachings. Jesus brought clarity out of confusion.

It is our job to do the same thing in our world, to remind those around us of what God is really like, who He really is.

Out of a sincerity to do exactly that, there have been movements to "be weird," or be radically different, or live in a way that makes people question why you do what you do. I totally get the idea behind these campaigns, but I believe they are overcorrections to the apathetic way some Christ Followers live.

It seems there are two extremes: either a Christ Follower lives so similarly to everyone else that there is no indication of Christ in that person's life whatsoever, or they intentionally go to the other extreme and live so "weirdly" that they become off-putting. When people who don't share our faith meet Christ Followers who fit in these categories, they walk away with one of these thoughts: "That person's relationship with Christ is meaningless" or "That dude is weird."

Where in the Bible does God instruct us to be weird? Sure, I believe He wants us to be different. But weird? Jesus didn't think, "Hmm…what can I do that's going to be scandalous?" Instead, I believe He thought, "What can I do that is going to show everyone the true nature of my Father?" I remember us being called to be salt and light (Matt. 5:13). We're called to be Christ's witnesses (Acts 1:8). We're called to be a city on a hill (Matt. 5:14). In short, we're called to a higher standard, not a weirder standard. We're called to show love, joy, peace, patience, kindness, goodness, gentleness, faithfulness, and self-control.

6/28/16

As I'm nearing the end of *The Brothers Karamazov*, I find myself more and more pondering the comments Dostoevsky, through Zosima, made about technology. He postulates that the purpose of technological advancement is to create a quicker transmission of thought, with a goal of uniting the people. But Zosima argues that the opposite will actually happen, that it will only create isolation.

One only has to experience social media on a small scale to realize how accurate Dostoevsky's 130-year old prediction is. Blogs, Twitter, Facebook – they only further entrench our beliefs rather than open our minds. They make us pursuers of winning an argument rather than discoverers of truth. We'd rather be validated than informed and enlightened.

Social media may plant seeds of knowledge, but it will never plant seeds of compassion. I have met people who have credited books as life-changing; however, I have yet to meet anyone who credits life change to a social media share or as the result of a debate.

Perhaps quicker transmission of thought leads to less reflection of thought.

6/30/16

The more I think about that last statement, the more I believe it. Think about how the news is driven right now. By clicks, views, some sort of consumer metric (click-bait). And why? Because those metrics mean advertising dollars. And how do you increase those metrics? By being the first to report on something. And since there will always be someone looking for the next thing to be first to report on, the life cycle of a news story is greatly reduced. The Orlando shooting seems to already be old news, insensitive as that may sound.

This quick consumption of news and quick turnover of news stories leaves no time for reflection and has the unfortunate side effect of leaving us as a numb, calloused, desensitized people.

No empathy.

No compassion.

I'm convinced that grief is a spiritual practice that we are quickly moving away from. Consider how the posture of grieving contrasts from the posture of control. Solomon claims there is a time to mourn (Eccles. 3:4), which means that mourning has its necessary place in life and, thus, its necessary role.

One could certainly argue that technological advancements have deepened the division among the world's inhabitants, and I think that it is largely due to our deep-rooted need for control. Even if one is reluctant to put the blame for division on the shoulders of technology (in particular, social media), I don't know that anyone would credit technology for further uniting the world.

7/6/16

I finished *The Brothers Karamazov* by Fyodor Dostoevsky on Saturday, July 2nd. There is much to discuss. First, the fruit of love. More specifically, the story of Alyosha and Zosima. Zosima was a monk who never expected to be a monk. He had done something terrible and followed that up by assaulting his servant. This act filled him with regret and caused him to repent. He eventually became one of the most influential monks of his monastery due to his overwhelming ability to be compassionate. The other elders (especially Father Ferapont) had a bit of an air of self-righteousness about them. Zosima experienced humanity, humility, and suffering. His dying instructions to Alyosha were to leave the monastery, to marry, and to minister to the world in that way. He himself, though weak and dying, poured out all his energy for those who needed him. I think Zosima knew that to be effective in ministry, one has to know what the people are going through on a personal level.

Alyosha has two brothers: Ivan and Dmitri. The bulk of the story revolves around Dmitri's sour relationship with his father, Fyodor. Fyodor is murdered in the book, and Dmitri is interrogated and arrested for this crime. However, it is the character Ivan that intrigued me. He doesn't believe in God, or at least he believes that he doesn't believe. His conversations with Alyosha and even the Devil indicate his problems aren't really with his belief in the existence of God as much as they are with organized religion and, perhaps, the nature of God as he understands it. For instance, if God were as good a being as the church states that He is, why do so many injustices occur in His world?

Things aren't so different now as then. The same struggles appear even today. A question that plagues us now is merely an echo of what plagued Dostoevsky over a hundred years ago. Is there a God? If not, is there a truth? A right or wrong? Ivan persisted that there is no God, and thus, "everything is permissible," but when he was confronted with wrong, he was overwhelmed with guilt and regret. The conflict in his mind drove him literally crazy.

We realize internally what is right (which I think the word righteous refers to) and what is wrong.

Ivan said that one has a duty to be selfish if there is no right or wrong because that is the best way to live. But once we experience the guilt and regret from our selfish actions, we can no longer deny that right and wrong in fact exist. Right and wrong are no longer opinions or cultural best practices but facts and universal truths that are the foundations of how we are made individually and how we exist in community.

7/8/16

Yesterday five police officers were murdered in Dallas, Texas. These are the moments where I am at a loss. These are the moments when people ask the same questions they've asked since Dostoevsky's time: Is there a God? And if so, why does He allow so much evil? I think of the babies Dostoevsky wrote about being murdered in front of their mothers many years ago, and I think about police officers murdered only yesterday.

The world many times seems hopeless. With two children and one on the way, it is easy for me to get scared. But Christ repeatedly said not to be afraid. For the purpose of evil is to cause fear, but 1 John 4:18 says that perfect love drives out fear (I believe Zosima referred to this as active love).

Love drives unity. Fear drives isolation.

Fear can crumble a nation.

Even though I whole-heartedly believe this, why is it difficult for me? Because fear (like evil) is very real and very strong. And it must be fought with perfect, active love.

Fear fights evil with evil.

The Spirit fights fear and evil with love, joy, peace, patience, kindness, goodness, gentleness, faithfulness, and self-control. Zosima's dying words instruct us how to respond to evil with compassion.

> "And even though your light was shining, yet you see men were not saved by it, hold firm and doubt not the power of the heavenly light. Believe that if they were not saved, they will be saved hereafter. And if they are not saved hereafter, then their sons will be saved, for your light will not die even when you are dead. The righteous man departs, but his light remains. Men are always saved after the death of the deliverer. Men reject their prophets and slay them, but they love their martyrs and honor those whom they have slain. You are working for the whole, you are acting for the future. Seek no reward, for great is your reward on this earth: the spiritual joy which is only vouchsafed to the righteous man. Fear not the great nor the mighty, but be wise and ever serene. Know the measure, know the times, study that. When you are left alone, pray. Love to throw yourself on the earth and kiss it. Kiss the earth and love it with an unceasing, consuming

love. Love all men, love everything. Seek that rapture and ecstasy. Water the earth with the tears of your joy and love those tears. Don't be ashamed of that ecstasy, prize it, for it is a gift of God and a great one; it is not given to many but only to the elect."[2]

Chapter 6

July 2016

The Voice of God Project

7/12/16

I have been writing a lot about *The Brothers Karamazov* in the month of July, but since Sunday, July 3rd, I have been reading *Gilead*[1] by Marilynne Robinson. It is a story about an old preacher in Iowa named John Ames who finds out he is dying. He has a young son, and he decides to take time to write his story to his child.

I love the way the old man writes his memoirs. When I first read the beginning where the narrator says he has a short temper that he struggles to control, I thought that the spiritual fruit that would be my focus this month would be self-control, but in reality, the book speaks mostly of peace, and, in a way, it speaks to how meekness is an important seed to plant.

This preacher is so interesting in how zealous he is internally, but how meekly he expresses himself.

7/17/16

Last night I watched the movie *My Life*[2]. It is a wonderful movie. Even though it's been a while since I've seen this movie, I've thought about it a lot while I've been reading *Gilead*. The premise of each work is very much the same.

A man in the prime of his life finds out he is terminally ill. His career is going well, his wife is pregnant, his life is perfect…except that it is going to end soon. I'm a huge Michael Keaton fan, and he plays the main character, who uses a camcorder to teach his unborn son life lessons that he will miss out on.

Something that has bothered me since I became a father is the thought of what would happen to my family if I left this world unexpectedly. Who would take care of them? It is a thought that continues to haunt me, especially now that I have a third child on the way. But *My Life* has helped me to see that they would be okay. And *Gilead* has reminded me that God Himself loves my wife and children even more than I do. I love the part in *Gilead* when John Ames addresses this indirectly:

> "Why do I love the thought of you old? That first twinge of arthritis in your knee is a thing I imagine with all the tenderness I felt when you showed me your loose tooth. Be diligent in your prayers, old man. I hope you will have seen more of the world than I ever got around to seeing – only myself to blame. And I hope you will have read some of my books. And God bless your eyes, and your hearing also, and of course your heart. I wish I could help you carry the weight of many years, but the Lord will have that fatherly satisfaction."[3]

I asked Julie what themes you could pull from *My Life* if you had to lead a class on it. We came up with the fragility of time (numbering your days), forgiveness, and prioritization of what matters. I love when the main character accepts the Chinese healer's words that he is going to die; the cancer is too aggressive. He asks the healer what he should do, and the healer tells him to put his life in order (he actually says, "Put your house in order," but he points to his heart, the man's house).

Another theme would be regret. When Bob Jones (the main character) was a boy, he had a dream of seeing the circus. However, his father was never able to give his son this opportunity. The relationship between Bob and his family deteriorated as he got older, and it seemed as though it could never be repaired. However, when Bob's family found out he was dying, his father got a second chance to make his son's dream come true by having the circus perform right on Bob's lawn. "Better late than never," Bob's father whispered as his son watched the performers.

Perhaps living wisely is easier than I originally thought. At least the concept. A wise life is one that mitigates regret. That may sound too simplistic, but wisdom truly is simple. Can you imagine if the son had died unexpectedly? The father would have missed his opportunity to do something special for his son, and the resulting regret would have eaten at him every day the rest of his life.

Regrets stay with us until our very last day. Sometimes they are obvious; sometimes they are not. Perhaps Bob's father once thought, *Oh, he'll get over it*. But it is obvious that Bob's father himself did not get over it. It makes me wonder what am I doing in my life currently (or perhaps, what am I not doing) that I will one day regret?

7/23/16

It is hard for me to say exactly what I loved about *Gilead*. Maybe it is just the complete understanding John Ames has about life, people, relationships. Maybe it's the way he searches for understanding, like when he's trying to figure out why he's so upset with Jack Boughton, the son of his dearest friend. Maybe it's the way he is so committed to moderation, which seems to help him stay meek, to not overreact as a parent, and to bear others in love. Maybe it's his empathy. Maybe it's his transparency. Maybe it's the life of peace that I imagine he lives. Maybe it's the way he won't enter into debates with people about the existence of God and refuses to give proofs.

Maybe it's his trust in God and the power of prayer.

Perhaps it was good timing that I read this book. I was at the dentist the other day for my six-month cleaning. They want me to wear a mouth guard at night because I grind my teeth. Who can withhold grinding their teeth in this age? But Zosima and John Ames would ask me if I've prayed, if I've wet the earth with my tears. They would ask me why I am surprised by the behaviors of those around me, and then they would remind me of the goodness of God's creation.

7/28/16

Isn't it interesting that when we experience bad, our most common argument against it is that we don't want it? I've been thinking a bit about

Gilead and my conversations with my son, Caleb, about dying. Julie's great uncle died recently, and it was the kids' first time dealing with death; so, we've been talking about it a lot. When it hit Caleb that one day I would be gone, his reply (like all of our replies on this sensitive subject) was, "But I don't want you to die!"

What a moot point. Death cares not about our desires.

And yet there is something within us that desires life so strongly (for both ourselves and others) that it seems to our very core that denial of life (or theft of life) is indeed a great injustice. I wonder if anyone truly accepts it or if we're just fooling ourselves.

I guess some people would say the invention of religion is a device we humans have created to help us cope with death. I, on the other hand, believe we simply were not created for death, and at the core level (our soul) the agony we feel is our timeless particle wrestling with a domain that sets up limits we were never meant to experience.

Several years ago, I got a phone call at work. My mother called to let me know that my great-grandmother had passed away. I called my grandfather to tell him I was sorry to hear that his mother had passed. He seemed to be his usual self.

"Hey, Papa," I said. "Sorry to hear about Grandma Wagoner."

"Brandon, I'm glad you called," he said. "There is something I want to ask you. Would you mind being a pallbearer at her funeral?"

"Of course, I'll be a pallbearer," I said.

"Good, good. Listen, she's pretty heavy, and you're the only one. You think you can handle her?" he asked. I had a mental image of me dragging a casket across a cemetery while people watched, and I snickered. His humor is unique and hilarious. He seemed to be handling the loss of his mother well.

The morning of the funeral, I rode with my grandfather to the little church where the service would be. We left early so that we could get there before anyone else.

"Brandon," he told me as we drove along backroads, "I've now lost my father and my mother. Let me tell you something. When you lose your father, you lose a figure of stability, a person you can always count on to take control of a situation and help. When you lose your mother, you lose a best friend."

I loved listening to him as we rode, and when we got to the small church building, my grandfather was telling jokes with the little old ladies in the foyer. He was smiling and laughing, his charismatic self.

But then the two of us walked alone into the auditorium, and we could see my Grandma Wagoner's face. The sight of her in a casket completely changed my grandfather's demeanor. He didn't merely sniffle and wipe away a stray tear. He wept. He wailed. He had lost his mother, and it broke his heart.

I wish I could have seen the look on my face because I was in total shock. I had no idea he was going to break down like that. I mean, she was 89 years old. Surely, he knew she wasn't going to live forever. He had a long life with her around. So why did it seem to catch him off guard?

That is when I learned more about death than ever before. I realized that no one can ever prepare for death. There is no situation in which death is welcome. Sure, there are times when death brings an end to suffering, but we are never okay with its result.

It brought to mind my own future relationship with death. Even if my life goes perfectly, as well as it could possibly go, I will still eventually stand next to caskets that contain my grandparents, my own parents, my in-laws, etc. And one day, regardless of how perfectly my life goes, I will either stand next to a casket holding my wife, or she will stand next to a casket holding me.

It was at that point that I thought back to my grandfather's comment about losing stability when losing a father and losing a best friend when losing a mother, and I realized that you don't only lose that person. You lose a part of yourself.

7/31/16

In addition to reading *Gilead* this month, I also read *The Old Man and the Sea*[4] by Ernest Hemingway. I didn't read it so much as a fruit of the Spirit book, but more so just because I wanted to read it. It's very short and the perfect complement in length to the epic *The Brothers Karamazov*.

This work has spoken more about self-control than any other I've come across this year. The duration of the fight with the fish, the battling of the sharks, the pain that the old man had felt – all of this was achieved thanks to lengthy self-control. And yet, the fish was lost in the process. Still, there were personal victories, though at the cost of what little the old man had left.

I love the idea that this work is an analogy to Hemingway's writing career. It makes me realize that I have not shared his experience. I have not wrestled with my writing long enough to suffer with it.

It also makes me think about vulnerability and criticism. Writing has taught me so much about what it is like to be vulnerable. *What would someone think of this? Is this good? If someone says its good, are they just saying that? How do I know for sure it's any good? Is it too personal? Would it hurt any feelings? What are the comments about the work when I'm not around to hear them?*

Hemingway was obviously a great writer, but he was not always thought of that way by critics. I wonder if he would have been a writer in today's world. I don't see him doing book tours or maintaining a social media platform or anything other than writing. I think he wrote because he loved to write. And I admire that. He had stories in him that he had to get out.

Chapter 7

August 2016

The Voice of God Project

8/1/16

Yesterday I led our Sunday morning Bible class. My topic was legalism, but I really didn't want to discuss it. We all know what legalism is. So, instead I focused the class around what I thought is at the root of legalism. Too frequently we address and focus on symptoms instead of determining root causes and addressing them.

I hypothesized that legalism is a way to try to control one's salvation, which in turn fuels one's religious superiority over others. Originally, the Pharisees became legalistic in order to please God and keep His commands. However, this practice, noble as it was during its inception, turned into a way for the Pharisees to take salvation out of God's hands and put it into their own hands. Taking this further, the Pharisees almost had an air about themselves as if they had God in their debt.

We all have a need for control, some more than others. And control, which drives legalism, is rooted in fear, and this is where we spent the bulk of the class time. Obviously, fear has been on my mind quite a bit as of late, and I feel that our nation in particular is grappling with this right now.

I am starting to think that all evil is rooted in fear. When I say evil, I mean *anything* not good, not perfect, not as He designed it. The word choice may seem strong, but when you consider the fall from the ideal world and the pain we suffer as a result of that fall, I wonder if it isn't actually quite appropriate.

But wait! I thought that some behaviors are an attempt at pleasure! How is that rooted in fear?

Yes, I think the selfish, pleasure-seeking, all-consuming lifestyle is a form of evil (not on the same spectrum as all the evil we see on the news, but not behavior from God). I also think that behavior is rooted in fear. Fear of dying (YOLO!), fear of missing out (Eve and the fruit), fear of loneliness, fear of wasting life, fear of being forgotten, etc.

Jesus says something like, "Do not be afraid", "Fear not", or "Take courage" one hundred twenty-five times. But how many times do we hear that in church? How many times do we tell ourselves that? I always felt a little uncomfortable about Christ's commands to not be afraid because I wondered how one can help being afraid. But I think perhaps Christ was making the same point that President Roosevelt was making in the quote I referenced earlier.

In other words, I think Christ was saying, "Don't let your fear control you. Don't give in to evil actions. Don't let evil win. Don't let evil change who you are; when it slaps you across the cheek, stand firm and run the risk of your other cheek being slapped."

I think Christ's comments are as much about faith as they are about fear, and in the class yesterday we discussed how fear and faith are mutually exclusive. Once, when Jesus calmed the storm, He told everyone not to be afraid. He then immediately asked them where was their faith. Thus, we can conclude that fear and faith cannot be present simultaneously.

Faithfulness will be my fruit this month.

Too many times I've mistaken faith for confidence, when I should have thought of it more like courage. In fruit terms, perhaps faithfulness means not panicking.

To close out the lesson, we looked at the Mount of Transfiguration. Peter saw Moses and Elijah, and he started talking about building shelters: trying to take control of the situation. While he was talking, God spoke up, which terrified the apostles. They fell to the ground, cowering in fear. I love what followed after Jesus told them to not be afraid and to get up.

"When they looked up, they saw no one except Jesus." (Matt. 17:8)

Looking for Him and seeing only Him can comfort our fears.

Last weekend, my company hosted a booth at a local Bluegrass Festival. The guy in the adjacent booth came over during a slow time and introduced himself. We got to talking, and he told me he was from Florida. I asked him what brought him to Nashville. "God," he said, and then he told me about how God changed his life. Not in a pushy way or anything, but just conversationally.

A few weeks ago, I took my van to get some new tires. It was going to be a while, so I got my copy of *The Brothers Karamazov* and started walking toward the mall adjacent to the shop to get something to eat. As I walked past Target, a guy ran out the store and chased me down to talk to me about my "Bible." He was sitting at the coffee shop inside and saw me walk by and left everything to come out and meet me. I explained that what I was carrying wasn't a Bible, but as we talked, I found out he travelled from Texas to minister to kids at the rodeo that was in town. I was a little nervous when this guy I didn't know was chasing me down asking me, "Hey! Why are you carrying that Bible?" But when I left, I thought how odd it was that he felt the need to seek me out. Certainly, he was very different than me. He dressed differently, spoke differently. He was probably someone I would not have thought had anything in common with me, but it was as if God wanted me to see that this man was my brother in Christ.

A few years ago, a man stopped me in an airport to tell me he is also a Christ Follower (he had seen the book I was reading at the time – it's funny how carrying a book around can get you into these conversations). We spoke for a while before the airline started boarding the plane. When we parted ways, he told me he'd see me "upstairs." I know one day he will.

Perhaps these kinds of experiences are my own Mount of Transfiguration moment. Perhaps they are God's way of telling me to stop trying to control things, to get up, to stop cowering in fear, and to see Him. Only Him. Right in front of me. Perhaps that is His way of comforting my fears, and reminding me He is still alive and working.

August 2016

8/7/16

For the month of August, I am reading Viktor Frankl's *Man's Search for Meaning: An Introduction to Logotherapy*[1]. To say it is a difficult read is an understatement. I cannot believe that one person could treat another in such a way. Frankl went to Auschwitz with his parents and pregnant wife. His wife would die without his even knowing. As the Jewish men, women, and children would depart the trains at the concentration camps, they would be briefly visually inspected, then directed one of two ways: work or chamber. With the wave of a finger, the Nazis would determine life or death.

Even though this spiritual journey is supposed to focus on love, joy, peace, patience, kindness, goodness, gentleness, faithfulness, and self-control, I feel like I have spent the last few months pondering fear. Then I pick up Frankl's book, and I am blown away by the terror these people must have felt every moment of every day for years. It makes me reconsider my earlier statement about fear and faith being mutually exclusive. How could someone not be afraid, even full of faith, in those situations?

But then I think of Christ in the Garden of Gethsemane. He was so afraid that He was sweating blood (Luke 22:44). Who would have more faith than Christ?

But upon further consideration, it is Christ's behavior that proves that faith and fear are mutually exclusive. He could have rescued Himself, which would have been an action driven by fear. Instead, He remained faithful to His Father, even to the point of giving up His own life.

8/16/16

Frankl makes a comment that there are only two races: decent and indecent. His comment is extremely relevant as race relations have gone backwards as of late. Racial tensions appear to be at the highest point of my lifetime. I have spent some time considering Frankl's comment, and it seems a bit controversial to me. I can't quite figure out why that is, though.

Perhaps it seems too simple. I've been made to believe race is a complex subject, and I agonize on how I'm going to raise my children to respect people of all different backgrounds and cultures. But I believe Frankl's comment shows me how to do that. By teaching my kids to think of people as merely decent or indecent, hopefully they will see people that are different than them as God's beloved children.

But can this concept be enough to heal a divided nation? I'm skeptical, but I believe it is the appropriate first step. If Frankl, a Jewish concentration camp survivor, can see decency in the occasional camp guard, I at least feel hopeful for our world.

8/29/16

I finished *Man's Search for Meaning* by Viktor Frankl. I got the idea to read this book during our annual unified service where several local congregations meet together for a lesson and a meal. The guest preacher spoke about empathy. He was an African-American preacher who had spent time in the school system and had a proven track record of helping young men, particularly those who are minorities. He gave examples of ways we can try to put ourselves in the shoes of other people. He mentioned several books and authors, and one name I remembered him saying was Viktor Frankl. I'm so glad he mentioned him because I feel like *Man's Search for Meaning* is one of the most well-written works I've come across, and it is perfect for the spiritual journey I'm trying to complete.

I wish I could quote the entire book, but, of course, I cannot. Everyone should spend time reading this work of Frankl's, though. I cannot recommend it enough.

Frankl wrote extensively about suffering, injustice, revenge, love, freedom, hope, courage, responsibility – and above all, our individual calling, our individual meaning.

To pick out one quote from this book is a nearly-impossible task. There is the scene where the prisoners took a moment to be in awe of the sunset, the comments about tears and courage, the story of Frankl's decision to stay behind and help his fellow Jewish prisoners when he had a chance to escape. But perhaps the quote that I believe is most timely for our world is the most practical and maybe most simple yet radical comment in the entire book:

> ...no one has the right to do wrong, not even if wrong has been done to them.[2]

8/31/16

Julie and I are leading a Life Group at our church, and since we decided that we are going to take a break from leading at the end of the year, I decided to do my own Life Group curriculum on *Forrest Gump*[3]. I've had this idea for quite some time, and I decided to be a little vulnerable and roll it out to the group to see what their thoughts were.

I'm also starting to gradually accept this crummy old world and relieve myself of the responsibility to fix it. I credit much of this to meeting Papye, of whom I'll write more of later.

The curriculum I'm developing on *Forrest Gump* is really fun. It basically looks at the movie as a parable. In this very imperfect analogy, Forrest is this God or Christ figure, and those that he interacts with are symbolic in their own way. No, it isn't perfect, but I do believe that the way Forrest interacts with some people is similar to the way God interacts with some of us.

Bubba is like the soil that immediately takes hold of the seed. Immediately, Bubba and Forrest hit it off and became good friends. Bubba was comforted by Forrest as he was dying in Vietnam. In fact, Bubba asked Forrest, "Why did this happen?" as his life was slowing slipping away. This is a question we often ask God. It is interesting to think about Bubba dying. If Forrest would have found Bubba first, he probably would not have gone back to save the others. So, as our group pondered whether or not Forrest had saved Bubba, we realized that in order for the other soldiers to be saved, Bubba's life would have to be lost. In other words, Bubba lost his life for a reason: to save the other soldiers. We often tell ourselves that things happen for a reason, and this was an interesting example of how sometimes the reason is not obvious.

We studied Lieutenant Dan as a representative of a person who believes his life has a specific meaning. He had his life mapped out, and there was a certain legacy he expected to leave. (This is certainly timely in my spiritual journey as I have spent a lot of time wrestling with control). However, when things didn't go the way Lieutenant Dan expected, he struggled to find meaning in his life. He felt worthless, and worse, he felt useless. He believed he was destined once for great things, but no longer. Forrest saw Lt. Dan as valuable as he ever was, and it was when Lt. Dan finally had a knock-down, drag-out with God that he came to terms with his lot in life. And he found peace in a life he wouldn't have expected, but was undeniably good. It is significant that it was Forrest himself that rescued Lt. Dan and in doing so, removed the possibility of the legacy Lt. Dan had lived for.

Of course, Jenny is the most explicit example of God's love. She was a person who consistently pushed Forrest away. She saw his lifestyle and could not accept it, could not adopt it. Sure, he had provided encouragement and peace during her youth, but as she grew up and changed, he remained the same. The world was a complex place, and he didn't seem to understand it. However, he never stopped pursuing her. No matter what she did, he couldn't love her any less. And finally, one day she realized that she didn't deserve him. She visited him and started to share life with him, but shame kept her from committing her life to him. It wasn't until the end that she finally gratefully accepted his love and became his bride.

No analogy is perfect, but I do believe that our study of *Forrest Gump* as an analogy to God's character has helped us somewhat to learn more about His nature.

Chapter 8

September 2016

The Voice of God Project

9/17/16

Okay, there is no book this month, and that is completely intentional. It is the result of a recurring dream I had in August. This dream made me rethink some things that I was doing during this spiritual journey. I have now had two vivid dreams during this journey, and while I'm not willing to say that I'm certain that those dreams are God's way of communicating to me, I'm also not willing to say that I'm certain God is not trying to communicate to me through those dreams. First, I will describe the dream; then I will tell what it taught me; and finally, I will tell of my experience in September.

I dreamed I was walking the streets of a big city, probably the Manhattan area. It had been raining, but now it was over. Shop owners were moving water and cleaning up the mess that the rain had left behind. I was with my friend (I don't remember who), and as we walked, he talked, but I didn't really listen. I was too busy watching everyone else.

We came to a short, bald guy who was from another country, possibly India. He is how I would describe a monk to be, maybe a retired monk (if there is such a thing) because he just wore jeans, a plain dark tee shirt, hiking sandals, and glasses. He also had the solemn personality of a monk, something you could tell about him immediately. He had a big cargo van, and he was taking books out of the back of it and arranging them on a table with his dog's leash tied to one of the table legs. His dog was small and quiet, but excited. He was going back and forth investigating everyone who passed by, not unlike myself.

I can't walk by a bookstore, even a mobile street vendor bookstore, without stopping for a look. So, I browsed the titles, but I was really more interested in the old man. Finally, we started talking. I don't know what started it, but I remember talking about books. I told him my favorite book, and I remember finding out his name: Papye Sa'je. Funny enough, I don't remember him telling it to me, though. Our discussion turned from books to philosophy, though I don't remember any details from our conversation.

What I do remember is my friend repeatedly trying to pull me away from my conversation. He was ready to go, but I wasn't. But it was impossible to continue having the conversation with Papye because my friend started physically pulling me away. I had questions and was searching for answers. I felt like Papye had answers, but my friend was going to keep me from hearing them. My obligation was impeding my journey. Finally, I said goodbye to Papye, never expecting to see him again, and went with my friend. My opportunity seemed to be lost.

However, the next night (at least in my dream it was the next night), I had the same dream. It was raining again. I was walking the streets of the big city again. But this time I was alone. I began to look for Papye's bookstand, and I was not disappointed.

We picked up our conversation right where we had left off. This time I could really enjoy it since I didn't have someone pulling me away. In fact, we spoke so long that it became time to pack his books up. In the late night, still wet from the evening shower, I wanted nothing more than to be there with Papye and his dog as we packed up his van. I didn't want our time to be over. When he was finally all packed up, table and all, he invited me to ride with him.

As I got into the van's passenger seat, I saw a book sitting on the armrest between the two front seats. When I looked at it, I realized it was the same book I had told him was my favorite the evening before. I asked him his thoughts about it, and he told me he read it since I recommended it to him.

"What did you think of it?" I asked. "Isn't it so full of wisdom?"

"It's okay," he said as he started up the van, "but it is not where to find answers."

He started driving, and I didn't know where he was going. We rode in silence. It was dark outside, and the darkness outside mixed with the quiet inside.

It's hard to explain what happened next. I let the darkness and the silence envelope me. I took it all in. I wasn't tired, but I felt like I was going to sleep. No, that's not right. I was fully aware. I felt like I was watching myself go to sleep. Maybe the best way to explain it is that I felt myself being driven into a dream by Papye. It was as if he was directing my thoughts.

It was so dark I couldn't see anything outside the windows of the van. Then a sound broke the silence. It was a woman crying. She wasn't crying hard, but she was sobbing, sniffling, obviously trying to stop the tears but not able to do so. Outside the van, the darkness lifted, and I could see the woman. Her back was to me. The way she held her head in her hands and wiped at her eyes was familiar to me. She had the posture of my mother.

Then another sound was heard, another voice. I could hear the unmistakable voice of a little boy. He was saying, "It's okay momma. Don't worry about me. I'm going to turn out okay. I'm going to be just fine."

When I turned to look at the boy, I was struck to see the kitchen in the house I grew up in. It was exactly the same, perfect to a detail I couldn't have ever remembered so clearly. The yellow stove, the linoleum floor, the dark cabinets where we used to set mice traps, the big TV in the living room (a tube set with decorative wooden trim and two rotary knobs at the top right), and all the wallpaper patterns that I had forgotten long ago surrounded me. It was like stumbling upon a repressed memory so vivid that I nearly felt I had gone back in time.

Then I turned my attention to the boy who had spoken. He was standing on the threshold of the living room to the kitchen. The woman stood near the stove, facing away from the boy, obviously trying to hide her emotions from him. There was something cooking on the skillet, and

I didn't have to see it to know it was a grilled cheese sandwich, something she made for me all the time.

And then there was me. I was the boy. He (I) was standing on his tip toes, talking to my mother, reassuring her, trying to convince her. Then little-me turned his attention to me. I looked myself right in the eye and he said, "They're going to be okay, too. Don't worry about them."

I wanted to know more. Was he talking about my children? As a father, I can't help but worry about my kids, and my anxious attitude, especially during this strange time in our world, makes my worrying worse. But before I could ask, my surroundings changed.

I was being led into a bedroom by Papye. It was my parents' old bedroom from our house on Grandview Circle. Everything was the same except for the bed, including the hollow door that had a hole in it where it bumped into the corner of their dresser as it opened. Papye was showing me around, but I couldn't take my eyes off the bed in the center of the room. It was so tall, so far off the ground. I asked Papye why, and he told me, "It is what is under the bed that is important, not what's on top." I looked underneath the bed at the empty space. I told Papye that there was nothing under there. He said he couldn't have me talk that way. He said that everything was under there.

Before I had a chance to follow up and ask Papye what he meant, our surroundings changed again. This time I was looking on at two men who appeared to be in the middle of an intense argument. I had the sure feeling that they could not see or hear me. I was just there as a witness. It was obvious that one was submissive to the other. In fact, I had a feeling that one was servant to the other. The servant had been offering some advice to the other man, but the other man obviously didn't want to hear it. He was yelling at the servant in reply, so hateful toward him. I don't remember the conversation or the topic, but I do remember that the advice was sound. It was wise.

I asked Papye who the man was. It appeared the entire scene happened many years ago. Did I descend from the man? I was afraid of Papye's response.

He said the man was no one, but that he was everyone. So, no, I did not descend from that particular man, but yet every man descended from such a man.

I asked why the man was being so hateful and yelling at the servant. I pointed out that the servant was just trying to help and that the advice was good.

Papye answered that the man just saw the servant merely as physical help and not intellectual help. Papye explained that the man thought the servant could not offer anything intelligent.

I said, "But the servant was right! The advice he gave was good!"

"Yes," Papye answered, "but he refuses to listen because of the servant's status. He is very likely to follow the bad advice of another man in another position in life. But we are all born in the truth. It is a part of us all. Everyone has the ability to speak truth, regardless of background or status."

I thought on this for a moment, and a question came to mind. "This is everyone?" I asked. "Then it happens all the time?"

Papye's expression confirmed my suspicion.

The next night I once again dreamed I was walking the evening sidewalks of a big city. This time I made my way straight to Papye. I helped him set out his books. There were a million questions I had for him about all that I had seen the night before. Instead, though, I asked him about himself.

"Who are you? Did I make you up, or are you invading my dreams?" I asked.

"Who do you think I am?"

"I don't know. I don't even know what your name means."

"What do you think it means?"

"No clue. Maybe papal? Pope-figure? Sa'je is probably a play on sage, wisdom," I said. I had typed it into Google since my first dream, and it thought I was looking for papaya. I told him this.

"The answers aren't always on Google. You know that."

"Papal, father wisdom? Papye is close to baby. Maybe baby wisdom?"

"Which do you think is correct?" he asked me.

"None of those." I had the distinct feeling that I was not going to find out, at least not then. It felt certain, and so I changed the subject. "Why are you spending your time here?" I asked.

"What do you mean?"

"You know, with me. Why are you spending so much time with me? Selling yourself a little short, aren't you? You're pretty smart. Couldn't you be doing something a little more important than hanging out in my dreams?"

"Everyone exists for someone else," he said. "Some of us just accept that easier than others."

As we worked to set out books and run the store, I began to tell Papye about my year of studying the fruit of the Spirit and how I've used that as a way to structure a modern spiritual journey. I told him about all the books I had read. I guess I was subconsciously expecting him to be proud of me. I was surprised and stung when he finally spoke up.

"You thumb your nose at those people who you say are wrapped up in the consumerism lifestyle. You say they stream and binge-watch movies, get too wrapped up in sports, put too much stake and interest in social media, buy things they can't afford - all as a way to escape. It makes you so mad, and yet you do the exact same thing."

I was mortified and distraught at his words. I was quick to defend myself by saying that my goal was to understand and embrace the world, not escape it.

"Is that really what you are doing?" he asked. I thought for a moment. I wasn't sure.

"Are you sure you're not just escaping a broken world for an ideal one? Are you sure you're not just silencing the ignorant and disagreeable voices for the ones you admire and agree with?"

Now I was really not sure. That certainly wasn't my intention. Papye walked over to me and put his hand on my chest. I barely noticed him, I was so deep in thought. "I feel your water," he said.

"What does that mean?" I asked. My son had said that same thing to me the other day.

"The human body is 60% water. Sometimes it can be a peaceful river. Yours is a raging sea."

"You can't tell that," I said skeptically.

He took my hand and put it on his chest. I immediately understood what he was talking about. I felt his water and knew it was like a small pond whose surface was smooth as glass.

"Escape doesn't calm the waters. It just ignores them. You say everyone is brainwashed, that no one thinks for themselves, that they try to convince themselves (through others) that the waves inside them don't exist or are even pleasant," he accused. "Explain to me how your reading has been any different."

I had no response.

"Tell me," Papye said the next night as we organized books, "what is the answer to uniformity?"

"Diversity?" I answered.

"You say it like you're not sure."

"I'm not, really. But it seems like the right answer. Diversity seems like a worthy goal."

"Worthy, yes," he said as he set out more books. "But there is an even better, even greater goal: unity. Unify with those whose hearts are good, and diversity will take care of itself."

I was immediately reminded of Frankl's decent and indecent race comment. I believe Papye would break down people into two similar races: those whose hearts are good and those whose hearts are not.

"So how do you unify a world of broken hearts?" I asked.

"You cannot fix the world. Greater people than you have tried and failed. But you can work to heal your own heart, the only heart you can change. It will be good medicine to those around you, and perhaps others will slowly be able to heal themselves." His words made me remember the words of little-me as I convinced my mother I would be okay in my dream.

So, that's my dream. My wife asked me what I thought the part that involved my mother was trying to say. I think that is easy. My mother is a very strong woman. There are only a few times I ever remember her crying, but those memories are some of my most vivid. A son does not like seeing his mother weep. It throws off some sort of sense of justice, and righteous anger builds up against whatever is the cause of her sorrow.

It was as if in those moments she was coming to terms with her own strength. It was as if she was thinking, "I'm trying my hardest. I'm doing my best. And right now, my best doesn't feel like it's enough."

As a child, you think your parents can do whatever they want. The world seems simple, and so, any uncertainty on the part of your parents is very confusing. Now, as a father, I can understand those moments. I, myself, have lived those moments.

I think my dream was trying to convey comfort to me, in the same way I tried to comfort my mother.

I never figured out what it was under the bed, though. I was hoping for some answer. Under my own bed lie my degrees. Julie framed them for me after I finished graduate school, but since I don't have anywhere to hang them, they sit under the bed. Perhaps the dream was trying to tell me that learning is what is important. I don't know.

I've thought about this part of the dream a lot, and there seems to be some sense of finality that is attached to the bed. I thought about the phrase, "you've made your bed, now lie in it." I thought about the physical construction of a bed. I've built beds for both my son and my daughter, and the bulk of the design was around the legs and support frame of the bed, the part underneath.

Perhaps the bed in the dream is a symbol for the life I am constructing and the eternity to which I will one day enter into. Sometimes I get so frustrated with this world that I wonder if there is any point to any of it. Remember the phrase, "life stinks and then you die"? Well, I may not have uttered those words, but perhaps my attitude has reflected that sentiment at times.

I think Papye was trying to tell me that all of this matters. Every day, everything I do has some meaning and importance. I think Viktor Frankl would agree. Perhaps there are moments when I feel like I'm spending all my time on the frame of my bed instead of getting to the fun parts: the headboard, the fancy sheets, the duvet, the warm, inviting pillows. But it is the frame, the support, the legs that will keep me upright once I am asleep.

One day I will be gone from this earth. I think that what Papye was trying to tell me is that at that time, my soul will be thankful for the work done on the foundation, not so much for the decorations and beauty.

9/25/16

For the month of September, I decided that instead of reading, I should spend time praying. This decision was due to my dream at the end of August about Papye, which I've just described in detail. One thing I learned quickly is that I've forgotten how to pray. I always started out with this formula that felt much more like repeating than praying. It was so weird. I had all this stress and worry, all this anxiety. But when I tried to talk to God about it, I just couldn't.

This first became evident on Sunday, September 11th. I skipped church and went solo-sailing instead. I was excited to talk out my fears with God. I thought the tranquility of the lake would be a perfect environment for me to lay my burdens down. But you know what? It just reminded me of God's goodness, and all of my fears suddenly didn't feel so overwhelming anymore.

I felt the same thing when I went on our Leadership Wilson retreat at Sewanee September 22nd and 23rd. From the mountaintop looking down at the world below, all of the problems of the world took a completely different perspective. It occurred to me that it was the *proper* perspective.

In those environments, my prayers took on a tone of thanksgiving, even though my intention was a tone of pleading. I couldn't even do thankful praying easily. I still craved a formula. So, I stole an idea from Leadership Wilson, and early in the morning on Friday, September 23rd, I stood on a cliff and listed ten things I love about Julie, Caleb, Lucy, Sarah, and God.

I thought first about how beautiful Julie is. She really does get more and more beautiful all the time. Naturally, I thought next of Julie's love for her children and the selflessness she lives for every day. But then I thought about her and Nermin, her friend from Egypt. She took Nermin to the zoo earlier in the week. Nermin had never been. Julie took pictures of her and her daughter riding the carousel. I saw one of the photos on her phone. In it, Nermin was filled with complete joy. My wife did that for her. Nermin had texted Julie that night to say thank you. Julie is probably her best friend. She might be very lonely at times without my sweet and wonderful wife.

It was funny to me that when I started praying over the things about Caleb that I was grateful for, I started listing things that have gotten on my nerves in the past. His happy (and silly) demeanor, his running to me to hug (and jump and wrestle) me. He is wildly happy and lives every moment. I began to admire and miss his spirit. I thought about his heart and his willingness to forgive. I love the way his hair repels water like a duck's feathers. I love the way he calls me his best buddy.

I thanked God for Lucy's love for me. I love that she snuggles up to me and wants to be near me. I thanked Him for her humor and how stinking smart she is. She's so clever and cute. She doesn't care what anyone thinks of her. She's a natural leader. I love holding her sweet little hand. We're very similar, which sometimes can make things difficult between us, but also makes me think we might stay close as she becomes an adult.

How do you pick ten things to be thankful for about a person you've never met? That was precisely what I wanted to do for Sarah. I may not know much about her. In fact, I know nothing of her other than her name and gender, but there are some things that I do know: I will love to hold her precious tiny body. I will love to rock her, read to her, smell her sweet fragrance of youth. I will love to adore her in her cute onesies. I will love the sounds and involuntary movements she will make. Those are the things about Sarah of which I thanked God.

Finally, I told God the things about Him of which I am grateful, and it was in that way that I could express my fear, worries, and anxieties. I thanked Him for His power, and I was reminded that He is powerful enough to fix not only my personal problems but also the problems of this world. I told Him I was grateful for His willingness and ability to forgive. I'm grateful for His love and the way He pursues us. I'm thankful for His Spirit, for the goodness that He created, for His wisdom. I prayed to Him, "May your Spirit fill our country so that its citizens bear your fruit."

As I think of what I've learned about prayer this month, I think about Ernest Hemingway's comment about writing. It is reported that

September 2016

Hemingway once said, "It is easy to write. Just sit in front of your typewriter and bleed." I don't know if he really said that or not, but I think a very similar thing could be said about prayer. Prayer can seem intimidating, but really, it is easy to pray. Just bow your head and bleed.

Another time during the retreat at Sewanee, I saw a flowering leaf on the branch of a tree. It stood out to me, though there were hundreds similar that surrounded it. I wondered if anyone else had ever seen that particular leaf before. And if so, did he or she take the time to admire its beauty, as I was trying to do? I thought that the answer was probably no. You really had to go out of your way to get to this secluded spot. I wondered if maybe that leaf grew and blossomed just for that moment of me seeing it. As I thought about all that had to go into the creation of that blossom, which would not survive long and I alone may benefit from, I thought that its blooming was for a purpose, for a reason. I wondered if my witnessing of it gave it purpose. If God put things in motion, put life into that leaf, all because He knew I would see it.

What if God communicates to me like that all the time, but I just don't notice it?

What if God uses me as a way to communicate to others in a similar way?

9/28/16

I got up early last Saturday, and went out on my back deck to pray before the kids got up. Our family would be spending the entire day together, going to Granville Days followed by my niece's birthday party. I really didn't want to get upset with the kids since it was supposed to be a fun day. I have a habit of wanting to control them, and I really didn't want to do that. Sometimes it sneaks up on me if I'm not aware that I'm being controlling.

I prayed: "Help me to forget about all the negative today and just enjoy my family. If I wait for the world to be perfect before I'm happy, I never will be. Perhaps that's what joy is: being happy in spite of a broken world."

In my time of solitude that morning, I also had a thought about self-control. Self-control seems to be a spiritual fruit that doesn't mesh well with the others. It doesn't seem like it fits to me. Part of the reason is because I know people who reach out to Christ to get their life under control. However, they seem to not be able to kick their addictions many times.

Then I think about will power, and that just seems to go against the message of Christ. So, I thought that maybe self-control is really all about focus. I have a handwritten note that used to hang over my desk at work that read "You can only control yourself. Control yourself!" I wrote it when I first became an engineer because sometimes I would get emails or phone calls that would frustrate me, and I needed a reminder of what was inside of my control and outside of my control.

As I sat on my deck and contemplated self-control, I thought of that note. Perhaps that was what Paul was referring to.

Controlling yourself instead of others. Self-reflective, self-governing, self-aware, as opposed to governing others. Seeing the plank in our eyes as opposed to pointing out the speck in others.

I looked up the Greek for self-control in Galatians 5:23. It is *enkrateia*. Its root, kratia, means government. We get democracy from this root. Thus, a better definition for this word than self-control is self-governance.

This seems to go alongside the teachings of Jesus much better than my previous definition of self-control. When you look at several stories, including the story of the woman caught in adultery, who the Pharisees wanted to stone, Christ basically tells the Pharisees to worry about their own salvation and sins instead of hers (John 8:1-11).

Joshua perhaps gives the first example of this type of self-governance definition when he tells the Israelites in Joshua 24:15, "But as for me and my household, we will serve the LORD."

One should be sure to govern oneself (set his own boundaries), but avoid governing others (setting boundaries for other people).

Chapter 9

October 2016

The Voice of God Project

10/11/16

This month I am reading Ron Hall's and Denver Moore's book *Same Kind of Different as Me: A Modern-Day Slave, an International Art Dealer, and the Unlikely Woman Who Bound Them Together*[1], which is about a wealthy white man and a homeless black man that meet and the relationship that results. I'm not sure what made me read it because when I read the synopsis of it, I had really low expectations.

It feels good to be reading again. I've missed it. I like the book a lot, too. Race relations weigh on my mind frequently with all that is going on in our country. Charlotte, Dallas, San Diego, Colin Kaepernick, etc. Oh yeah, and the election. All of those and more have kept tensions high, and division strong among our nation's citizens.

I was so confused about what was right and what was truth. Twitter was where I was getting the bulk of my information about each of the events listed above. It is a double-edged sword because there is a lot of information shared there that is not available elsewhere. But people are so hateful there. Both sides of each argument were steeped in anger and thus, very biased. I reached out to Lamar and Taylor Moore to see their thoughts on it all. We made it our Life Group meeting.

In the Moore family, I see a family who loves God, has great character, and strives to be a family led by God's will. In fact, I feel like I have more in common with Lamar than I do with some of the white people I work with or even go to church with. They are people who I trust, and so I wanted to know their thoughts on all that was going on.

Many times, when people of different race backgrounds gather to talk about race, it becomes a debate instead of a conversation. I wanted to avoid this, and I think we were successful at that. Our discussion on Sunday, 10/9, was a good example of people trying to understand each other, not change each other's opinion.

This topic is so saturated with delicacy that it drips political correctness. I am so scared that I am going to say something wrong or ask a stupid question. I'm so afraid that in a sincere attempt to understand, I am going to come off as insensitive. I am so nervous that something is going to come out wrong, and I'm going to be thought of as racist.

I think political correctness, like legalism, had noble roots. Earlier, I wrote that legalism had a noble inception. After all, what is more noble than trying to do everything that pleases God at all times? But that is impossible, and eventually, legalism turned into a way to feel superior to others who weren't able to keep as many commandments, those who weren't perfect. In the same way, political correctness, I believe, had a noble inception. It was a way for us to be aware of the power of our words. It was a way for us to be self-aware of how we treat others. Political correctness showed us the impact of our language, and the goal was to treat everyone with dignity. However, political correctness, like legalism, has evolved into something very different than what it was intended to be. It seems to be used by some as a tool to catch people who misspeak. And then, instead of treating people with dignity, we ignore those who are different than us for fear of unintentionally misspeaking and mistreating them. Political correctness paralyzes us by fear, and some of us get so scared of messing up, we avoid entering into difficult discussions like this.

A tool becomes a hurdle.

Another reason I was a little hesitant to ask Lamar and Taylor to have this discussion with our Life Group is because I see them as more than just black individuals. They and their sweet son, Carson, are a family that my family wants to be close with. I want us to be friends. I have fun with Lamar, and I love to talk books with Taylor. I can be myself around them, and I think they can be themselves around me. I was afraid that if I approached them and asked to have a discussion about race, they would think, "Oh, here we go. We're hanging around this white family, and all they want to do is talk about how we're different."

But it wasn't that way at all. Lamar and Taylor were very gracious as I asked them some questions, and I wish the whole world could have witnessed our discussion. We both want the same thing: healing. We all want everyone to just treat each other right.

I really liked how Lamar closed the evening. He talked about how to go forward. That is where I struggle. I want to fix the world. I want to right all the wrongs. But I'm not Jesus, and even He couldn't/didn't do that.

Lamar shared his favorite verse with us as a way to guide us going forward:

"He has shown you, O mortal, what is good. And what does the Lord require of you? To act justly and to love mercy and to walk humbly with your God." (Micah 6:8)

10/15/16

I finished *Same Kind of Different as Me* last night. I read it in about a week and a half. It really was incredible. So timely, too. Ron Hall got into serving a local homeless shelter when his wife, Debbie, first wanted to get involved. During their work there, they met a man named Denver Moore. Ron and Denver reluctantly became friends, largely due to Debbie's insistence. She had a dream about Denver that God was going to use him, and Denver became good friends with Ron and Debbie's entire family.

I often slip into thinking that people who are so different (economic class and racial differences) cannot have a mutual relationship. I also tend to think people can't change who they are. Denver spent ten years in Angola prison. He was admittedly violent. And yet, his life ended up on a path no one (not even himself) would have suspected.

The parts of the book that I loved the most were also the parts I had the hardest time believing. There were several supernatural elements to the story, like when Debbie had visions of angels and her conversation with Christ. Then, the next day Denver stopped by and described the same scene to Ron without knowing what had happened. I want to believe those things are possible (like the story in 2 Kings 6:8-17 when Elisha prayed that his servant's eyes be opened and the man immediately saw a spiritual army). I actually think that deep down I do believe this, but it is difficult for me to admit it.

It seems to me that there was a phrase applied in this book that isn't very common practice today: benefit of the doubt. Denver's story seemed pretty far-fetched to me. I'm not sure I would have been able to believe it. But Ron and Debbie trusted him, and eventually Ron saw with his own eyes how honest Denver was about his story when the two of them took a trip back to Denver's home in Louisiana.

Another thing that amazed me was Denver's grace. His experience on the Man's plantation didn't burn him up in anger against the Man. In fact, sometimes he spoke very graciously about the Man. His experiences with some other whites left him fearful and distant. Perhaps there was some bitterness, but not nearly on the level one would expect or even deem acceptable, especially in a time where one word can have the power of triggering hateful response.

10/16/16

This month I have gone back to reading, but I haven't forgotten the words of Papye. Instead of reading to escape, I'm reading to engage. I'm having conversations with those whose backgrounds and experiences are different than my own. I'm listening not only to the authors of the books I've selected, but also to the people around me who may see the world in a very different way.

I've thought about my first dream of Papye, when my friend was trying to pull me away. I immediately thought that scene was a symbol that there are people in my life who may be preventing me from spending time learning from the one with all the answers. That may be true, but it has also occurred to me that the scene was trying to tell me that there are also people in my life who need me.

Maintaining that balance is hard, but Father Zosima showed me why it is important.

I've also thought about the song *Vita Nostra* that I wrote about earlier. The title means "Our Life", and in the scene of *The Mission*[2] when this song plays, there are two very different groups of people working together to do the will of God. I no longer think those drums, those maracas, and those voices are drowning out the oboe. The voices are singing along and the instruments are playing along with the original music, making music in their own way that complements the oboe. They aren't trying to prevent others from hearing God's voice; they are singing along with God in their own voice. They are making God's song their song.

And perhaps I've been taking the wrong approach of just trying to listen to the oboe instead of singing along.

10/25/16

When I was in graduate school, I had to take a couple of those personality tests for a class. I think those tests can be useful tools, but I've also been pretty critical of them at times because of how some people use them. The way our instructor used the results of the tests is a pretty solid example of what the tests were not intended for.

Around the classroom were several labels of the various possible outputs from the personality test, and every student was asked to find his or her label. I found mine and greeted the other students who tested the same way as myself.

Then the instructor went around the room to each group, stood apart from them and told them exactly what they were like. When she got to my group, she pointed at us and said things like, "You always do this; You never do that; You hate this; You love that; This makes you angry; That makes you happy; etc."

I was getting furious. She didn't even know my name, and yet she presumed to know everything about me and how I operate. Many times, her statements were wrong about me, but that wasn't what was really upsetting me. It was the pretentiousness. It was the box she was putting me into. It was the complete judiciousness without relationship. She thought she knew me because of some responses I gave on a test. She'd never even heard one word out of my mouth.

I've reflected on that night in class many times. It didn't take me long to realize that I actually do the same thing. Thinking back to *Same Kind of Different as Me*, I realized that had I been the one to meet Denver Moore instead of the Halls, I would have responded in a very similar way as my instructor. I would not have taken the time to get to know Denver. I would have seen one angry expression, one sneer, and that's all I would've needed to make my decisions about him.

But I'm starting to realize that people are complex. I'm complex. I don't think that personality test can completely understand who I am. I don't necessarily think that people fall into one of sixteen different categories or one of three different colors.

Denver is complex, too. Deborah Hall realized this. Her first impression of Denver was when he had an angry outburst and made a big scene, and yet she was convinced that he was someone special. She'd had a dream of him, and though the real Denver didn't seem to match the Denver she had dreamed about, she trusted that one instance did not rule out God's usefulness for Denver.

Thinking about this has made me realize I even do the same thing with Jesus. Speaking of complex personalities, think for a moment about the second chapter of John. In the first twelve verses, Jesus attended a wedding with His mother and His disciples (John 2:1-12). Imagine you also were a guest, or better yet, imagine you were one of the servants of the wedding. You happened to see Jesus intervene during a wedding crisis and help provide more wine when the host had run out. If you had never met Jesus before, you'd likely have a pretty high opinion of Him because of His actions at the wedding.

However, the following thirteen verses that make up the second half of the chapter show a very different side of Jesus. This is when Jesus went to Jerusalem right before Passover. He saw people trying to make money in the temple, and He drove them all out with a whip. He seemed pretty angry, and then He made a confusing claim that He could rebuild the temple in three days if it was destroyed (John 2:13-25). Imagine you happened to be visiting the temple on the same day, or better yet, imagine you were one of the money changers. You witnessed this entire event! If you had never met Jesus before, you'd likely have a completely different opinion of Him than someone who was at the wedding at Cana in Galilee. Perhaps you'd think He was an angry person, or maybe even crazy.

But I bet if someone told Jesus' mother, she wouldn't have been surprised. She knew how He was. She had a close relationship with Him. If someone were to ask her, "Which Jesus is the right one?" She'd probably say both. He is that complex. Yes, He loves to serve and help, but He is also passionate about His Father.

This complexity in the person of Jesus can be intimidating. How can I know how He would respond in certain situations when two consecutive stories show two very different sides of Him? Is it even possible?

I believe it is possible, but it's not easy. It takes time and a relationship. Consider Mary's exchange with Jesus at the wedding. Check out what happens in the third verse:

When the wine was gone, Jesus' mother said to him, "They have no more wine." (John 2:3)

That comment is innocent enough, right? "Hey Jesus, guess what I just found out. The wine is gone."

But look at how Jesus responds in the next verse:

"Woman, why do you involve me?" Jesus replied. "My hour has not yet come." (John 2:4)

That seems a little over the top, doesn't it? I mean, her comment was just a statement of fact, not a pleading for Jesus to intervene. At least, on the surface it seemed like an innocent comment. But we have to pay attention to the implicit dialogue going on. Remember, this is Jesus' mother. He knows her as well as any of us know our own mother, and he knows that the comment she makes isn't as innocent as it seems.

"Hey, Mom. I know you, remember? You can't pull one over on me. In fact, I know you so well, that despite your seemingly innocent comment, I know you are asking me to fix this situation."

But things get really strange in the very next verse. Look how Mary responds to Jesus' accusation:

His mother said to the servants, "Do whatever he tells you." (John 2:5)

In a normal conversation, a mother would have responded with something more like, "Hey, I'm not trying to involve you. I'm just letting you know."

Instead, however, Mary doesn't even directly respond to Jesus. She goes right to the servants and starts giving them instructions as if Jesus had told her get ready for the best wine she'd ever tasted.

But though she seemingly doesn't respond to Jesus, in reality, her remark is an indirect response to Him. He's her son, remember? She knows Him as well as any mother knows her child. And her reaction to His response says something very implicitly right back to Him.

It's as if she said, "Hey, Jesus. I know you, too, remember? You can't fool me. In fact, I know you so well, that even though your time hasn't come yet – and despite your discouraging reply – I know you are going to do this."

This conversation doesn't exactly add up unless you consider the implicit details. Here we have a mother and her son communicating to each other, the most important parts of this conversation being silent. Despite all indications showing that Jesus was not going to intervene, Mary knew better. She knew her son. She knew how He was going to respond. Even though the situation wasn't cut and dry (remember, His time had not yet come), Mary knew Jesus well enough to know His behavior.

This is the relationship I need with Christ if I am going to be able to bear His name successfully in the world I live in. It is this relationship that is going to help me to serve Him faithfully and to be a witness to others of His character.

Chapter 10

November 2016

The Voice of God Project

11/1/16

This month I am reading *The Ramayana: A Modern Retelling of the Great Indian Epic*[1] translated by Ramesh Menon, which is, the best I can tell, the Hindu New Testament.

Here is the background:

There was a demon named Ravana who was very self-centered. He was granted invincibility by a god named Brahma, but this invincibility only applied to gods and other spiritual, nonhuman beings. In other words, Ravana was not invincible to humans. He never thought to ask to be made invincible to human beings because he never thought a normal human could ever kill him.

Rama was a human prince born to King Dasharatha. He was the avatar (incarnation) of the god Vishnu. Rama married a woman named Sita, but one day he was exiled from the kingdom for fourteen years by one of his father's wives. Sita went with him into the wilderness, as did his brother Lakshmana. During this exile Ravana kidnapped Sita. Then Rama, along with Lakshmana and an army of monkeys, sought out Ravana's kingdom to rescue Sita.

The death of Ravana would save Sita, but Rama realized that by seeking out Ravana and killing him, Rama would also rescue the world of Ravana's evil dominion over it. Remember, only a human could kill Ravana, and it became clear to Rama and those around him that it was his mission to do exactly that.

It is remarkable at how Rama's character is valued and admired by every other character in the work (except the demons, many of whom are afraid of him). Menon even describes Rama as gentle, a fruit of the Spirit. The admiration of Rama's character speaks to a goodness that is so much a part of our human fabric, that our nationality or culture doesn't matter. This tells me that we are beings created to naturally know, recognize, and admire this type of goodness. If our existence is by accident and with no creator, how could different cultures gravitate toward the same ideas of good and evil, noble and selfish, right and wrong?

This is where I believe Robert Pirsig and myself differ. He traced the origins of quality back to Socrates. If that is true, then from that point on, quality and goodness become a learned trait of our culture, though subtly, almost subconsciously. This would not explain how other cultures obtained this same appreciation and admiration for goodness. In my mind, the only way to explain the universality of goodness is by recognizing all people of all cultures were created by the same Creator.

11/7/16

Tomorrow is the Presidential election. I'm so ready for this thing to be over. I've never felt more hopeless for our country than I do right now. I am hopeful that some of the division that is prevalent in our country diminishes once this election is over. I am hopeful that we can once again speak kindly to each other, regardless of our differences of opinion.

For months, I agonized over what I was going to do. The way I figured it, I had three options for my vote. I could vote for one of the two primary candidates or I could vote for one of the third-party candidates. Neither of the primary candidates really spoke to me. I'd watch the debates hoping for some sort of guidance, but I ended up turning them off feeling more dejected than ever. Some of the third-party candidates appealed to me, and I was leaning toward voting for one of them, even though I knew the chance of one of them winning was nearly zero.

Of course, I could also just not vote at all, but I will never do that. Too many people gave their lives to make this country the great nation that it is. They effectively fought for my right to vote. I will not waste that freedom that so many people around the world wish they had.

So, what could I do? I felt trapped. I felt like I had a problem to solve with no available answer. I kept waiting for some other option to appear from nowhere. Whatever choice I made, it occurred to me that I would have to look my children in the eyes and tell them that I did everything I could to protect and preserve their future and this country's future. I do not take that responsibility lightly.

But I had to do something, and last week when I showed up at the polls for early voting, I was prepared to do the one thing that I knew I could be at peace with.

I did not vote for either primary candidate. Nor did I vote for any of the third-party candidates. I mentioned that I take voting very seriously.

But I also take prayer very seriously.

So, when I got my ballot, I went into the voting box, punched "Write-in" and wrote "Jesus Christ". A friend had mentioned doing this, and I think he was kidding, but the notion stuck in my mind. I thought about the main responsibilities of the President. The way I see it, with the system of government we have in place, the President's main objectives are to lead the country in tone and attitude and to appoint Supreme Court Justices. I put my hope in Christ to do those things, and I believe He has the power to do so.

As I cast my vote, I took a moment to pray for my nation, the country my children will grow up in, the country that I hope my grandchildren will grow up in. I asked that God take over, that His will be done on Earth as it is in Heaven, that He not forget us or abandon us.

I turned my vote into a prayer, and as I took one last look at the name of my Savior as my choice for leader of this country, I felt a burden lift. I wanted to know that what I did made a difference, and I wanted to know that it was the right difference. I've never done that before in my past of voting for Presidents, and I doubt that I'll ever do that in the future. But it felt like the right thing for me at that moment.

And pressing submit on my ballot reminded me that no matter what, I cannot fix this world. Only He can. My vote matters.

My prayers do, too.

November 2016

11/15/16

There are so many things going on that I don't know where to begin this journal entry. Besides an election, protests (riots), a divided nation, a biased media, the beginning of the Thanksgiving and Christmas season, I also have a son who turned six years old and a baby girl who is about to be born any day.

I have thought a lot about *Same Kind of Different as Me*, especially in the aftermath of the election. Anywhere you look, people are talking about racism, fascism, bigotry, gender inequality, and profiling. I try to hear these messages through what I learned from Ron Hall and Denver Moore, as well as from my conversation with Lamar and Taylor Moore. It seems as though people largely think there are only two responses: 1) completely ignore those claims or 2) tear up stuff because those things exist.

I want to take a different approach. I like what Ernie Johnson said about looking in the mirror and trying to be a better man, about being a fountain instead of a drain[2]. My friend Wilson would say be life-giving.

Rama was mistreated when he was banished from the kingdom, and he was in disagreement with his brother, Bharata, who tried to convince him to stay as he was leaving. I believe I can learn something from the way Rama reacted in that situation, as well as his brother's plea for Rama to stay and rule.

Rama's brother, Bharata, was to be king of Ayodhya in Rama's place during the exile. But Bharata tried to convince Rama that it was really in Ayodhya's best interest if he stayed as king. Rama's father had died after the exiling of Rama, and Bharata was trying to convince Rama that he no longer needed to follow through with the exile. He was worried about what would happen to Ayodhya without Rama, and he expressed these concerns to Rama.

Bharata's comments to Rama about Ayodhya spoke to me because they so closely mimic my prayers about this election and its aftermath. My

Christian paraphrase version is: "America is a broken dream. Only you can put its pieces together again and heal our country. Accept our offering; it is for the good of everyone. The task is beyond us and not what we were born for. Help us, Jesus."

Rama's response to Bharata didn't appear to directly address Bharata's concerns, though. Instead, Rama spoke about time, death, relationships, uncertainty, and most of all fate[3].

How interesting it is to me that Rama embraces his grieving brother by speaking wisdom. The two are in disagreement, but there is one thing they can agree on: wisdom. Wisdom becomes a rock as they grieve their father and accept the hand that has been dealt them. Wisdom becomes a force that unites them as they disagree on how to move forward.

There is unity in wisdom.

11/18/16

Last night I met my daughter, Sarah. It was my third and final time to experience that awesome, miraculous feeling of anticipating meeting my child in the delivery room. My wife, who I admire now more than ever, was amazing. Sarah came abruptly, and there was no time for my wife to receive an epidural, a procedure she had been counting on. Nevertheless, she remained strong, and the love that shone in her eyes as she beheld her third child reminded me of how blessed I am that this woman is the mother of my children.

Caleb and Lucy, the big brother and big sister, came and visited Sarah today, and they are as smitten with her as I am. I am overwhelmed at the moment with joy and humility as I consider how gracious and good God has been to me and my family. I don't deserve this special life He has given me, but as I consider my role as father to these special children, I want to commit myself to their service. I want to live in a way that blesses their lives.

As I think about the adage that time passes quickly and that before I know it, my children will have been launched into the world, it terrifies me. I immediately try to find ways to slow time down. But since that is not possible, I realize the only thing I can do is to prioritize my children. It's not as easy to do as it is to say.

Raising kids properly requires a lot of self-denial. Sometimes the situations that require this are obvious, but sometimes they are not. I think about John Chapter 12, when Mary, sister of Martha, poured perfume on Jesus' feet, and Judas objected the action, saying that the perfume could be sold and the money given to the poor. Notice how Jesus replied.

"Leave her alone," Jesus replied. "It was intended that she should save this perfume for the day of my burial. You will always have the poor among you, but you will not always have me." (John 12:7-8)

Ever since having children, I've thought of this verse. Sometimes my priorities change as a result of having children, and that causes me to miss out on some good and noble practices. However, I have to remember that I will always have opportunities to serve (myself, my community, my organization, my church), but I will not always have opportunities to serve my children in the way that I currently do.

As I watch the gentle rising and falling of my daughter's chest, feel the soft, dry skin of her sleeping cheek, and listen to the tender, quiet whimpers of her voice, I am reminded of my mission as a father.

11/29/16

I finished *The Ramayana* last night. Well, I read the first six books, but not the last one, who many people say was written later. I read a couple summaries of it, and when I read that Rama banishes Sita, that confirmed to me that it was not worth reading. That is so unlike Rama.

The other night Julie started the Advent reading to the kids from *The Jesus Storybook Bible*[4]. It was eerie to listen to because parts of the introduction could have certainly applied to *The Ramayana*. "It's an adventure story about a young Hero…It's a love story about a brave

Prince who leaves his palace, his throne – everything – to rescue the one he loves."[5] Nearly the whole thing could have been an introduction to the story of Rama!

It brought to mind something I had read in the introduction of *The Ramayana* that Ramesh Menon wrote. He mentioned that all translations of *The Ramayana* that he had come across did one of two things: 1) It stressed the spiritual connotation and left out the narrative or 2) It summarized the events of the story and in the process, sacrificed any spiritual component. Menon argued that the text is more than a bland structure of rules regarding dharma and also more than merely a story.

The same can and should be said about the Bible. Something is lost when we categorize this sacred text in one of these two categories. Perhaps there has been a bit of over-correction by some to heavily focus on the story aspect of the Bible as a reaction to the incorrect focus on the text as merely a set of rules for so many years.

Dharma is the major theme of *The Ramayana*. I think some people would describe dharma as fate, but I personally think is more comparable to the will of God, this thought that everything happens for a reason. Rama gets banished so that he can kill Ravana. It isn't clear to him from the beginning, but this is his mission in life. Unfortunately, sometimes life deals us difficult situations in order to put us on our path to complete our mission.

If Ravana had never kidnapped Sita, Rama would never have had a reason to seek Ravana out.

"Things happen for a reason" is also a pretty prevalent theme in the Bible, and that is not the only similarity. One of the most fascinating quotes to me is where Sita is talking to Hanuman and says, "Rama always says that mercy and goodness are the only ornaments worth wearing. No one is sinless, Hanuman; let us be forgiving."[6] One could say that if one wore those ornaments, then a trail of goodness and mercy would be left in their wake throughout life. Then you could compare this to Psalm 23:6 where David says, "Surely goodness and mercy shall follow me all the days of my life."

I always thought David was saying that goodness and mercy were going to be the things he experienced throughout his life, but perhaps he was saying, "I am going to be good and merciful to those whose lives interact with my own, in such a way as my life will leave this trail of goodness and mercy in its wake."

Ravana was eerily similar to Pharaoh. Both knew that they needed to surrender, but pride kept them from doing so. Time and again plagues indicated that Pharaoh was no match for God. Time and again the deaths of Ravana's top warriors indicated he was no match for Rama. Both lost their sons. But both refused to relent. Pharaoh's heart was hardened every time he was about to lose the Israelites. Ravana's heart melted every time he saw Sita. Both of them let their hearts deceive themselves about their abilities.

Obviously, there is a lot that goes on in *The Ramayana* that is hard to believe. Reading it gave me a chance to see how some people may read the Bible and have difficulty believing some of the stories in it. In the Bible, the things that are hard to believe (miracles, people being healed, an ark full of animals, etc.) are the highlights of the narrative text. I think the authors expected that the audience would have doubts about those things. However, I feel that this is where there is a shift between *The Ramayana* and the Bible. The hard-to-believe things in *The Ramayana* (monkeys that can grow, leap across oceans, and rip mountains out of the ground) are almost conveyed nonchalantly, as if they are nothing out of the ordinary. It is Rama's character, his mercy, Sita's humility, Lakshmana's devotion, and all of their commitment to dharma that comes across as fascinating. I believe that reading this text has strengthened my faith in the events of the Bible because I have a new consideration of what is "hard to believe."

I don't exactly know my conclusion from reading *The Ramayana*. I think that perhaps (I'm not even sure I believe or feel comfortable in making this statement) it is a parable of sorts so that this culture could one day recognize Christ. Perhaps it was not meant literally but highly figuratively. I have a greater appreciation of spiritual warfare because of this text. This does not mean I believe in spiritual monkey-beings that fight for good. It means I feel like I better understand the magnitude of the spiritual battles that are going on all around me and the devotion of all that are fighting on both sides of that war.

Perhaps the phrase that best summarizes *The Ramayana* is uttered when Rama addresses his army on the eve of the great battle: "The hand of fate is always upon us, and everything that happens in this world is by fate."[7]

Even though Rama is described as gentle and his demeanor exudes peace, it is obvious to me that the strongest fruit of the Spirit that is evident in *The Ramayana* is faithfulness. It is amazing how much one can endure because of one's faith, though I think faithfulness is somewhat different. If faith is putting your trust into something or someone even though there exists no tangible certainty, then faithfulness is that trust in action. It is Rama submitting to his father to be banished for fourteen years. It is Christ drinking the cup of crucifixion.

So, the question I am struggling with is what does faithfulness look like for a Christ Follower in 2016? A bigger question is how am I being faithful and where am I not being faithful? I think we as Christ Followers (me included) have worried more about being winsome than being faithful lately. I look at Rama and how his faithfulness attracted people to him, but I look at Christ and see something different. Sure, He won many followers, but there were also those who disliked Him. And didn't He say the world would reject those who chose to follow Him (John 15:18-25)?

November 2016

I don't think there is anything wrong in appealing to the world (doesn't Jesus tell us to be the light of the world in Matthew 5:14-16?), but perhaps the problem comes when we do so and sacrifice faithfulness in the process. I'm thinking specifically about Jen Hatmaker's recent comments[8] right now, and though I can admire her heart for the world and her sincere attempt at reaching children of God that may have been ignored and/or excluded by the church, I also wonder if she hasn't sacrificed faithfulness in the process.

Being a Christ Follower doesn't mean everyone will love us. That would be nice, though, because we so desperately want others to see our love for them and to reciprocate it. But what do we do in situations where lifestyles conflict, where practices and beliefs are at odds? Isn't there a way to love someone and still disagree with him or her? How?

So, what is the right way? I think sometimes we read Paul's statement in Galatians 1:10 about trying to win the approval of God instead of men, and we immediately think that the two are mutually exclusive. Perhaps in some instances they are at odds with each other, but in other instances, perhaps there is a way to remain faithful but still show compassion.

Let me share a story where I've struggled with this.

A couple of years ago, Julie and I spent a week in Maine to celebrate our tenth wedding anniversary. One day, we were walking through some shops in Portland when we noticed a young man, probably around twenty or so, with a clipboard. He was approaching people and asking them to contribute financially to some program that he was involved with. I wasn't sure of the details, but when we overheard a fragment of his conversation with someone else, we realized that the program had something to do with his sexual orientation.

He seemed like a nice guy, but I was really hoping he didn't stop us. We were on vacation, and I was hoping we could just stay in our own little world for a bit longer before we had to return home to our kids and the madness of everyday life. So, I made a mental note to avoid him.

Funny enough, I made eye contact with the guy at one point as we were making our way down the sidewalk, and his expression seemed to convey to me his desire to avoid us, too. He probably took one look at us and realized we were pretty traditional people, and that his chances of getting a financial contribution from us was not very good.

(By the way, there are plenty of activities I would be hesitant to sponsor that involved heterosexual lifestyles, too.)

So, there was some mutual avoidance. That is, until Julie and I walked out of a bookstore and nearly ran him over. The three of us didn't see each other until we nearly collided. It would have been more awkward at that moment if the young man did not do his pitch; so, he started in.

"Good morning!" he said enthusiastically. He really did have a great personality.

"Good morning," we answered back.

"I'm involved in a program that works with high school students who are gay. As a part of that program, we offer counseling to these students. Some of that counseling helps them as they have questions about their sexuality and need someone to talk to, and some of the counseling is for students who are targeted by bullies because they are gay," he explained.

The whole time he was talking, I was praying silently, *Please help me to do this right. Please don't let me mess this up. There's a million wrong ways to do this. Please help me know the one way to do it right.*

The young man kept explaining about the program and how it costs money to get these counselors, which was why he was asking people for a contribution.

Then, all of a sudden, like a stealthy ninja from the shadows, out from nowhere some other guy appeared. He expertly moved between the young man and me and my wife, and as he walked by, he said something like, "Have you heard the good news about Jesus Christ?" And he passed us

November 2016

one of those tracts that look like a comic book. You've seen them. People pass them out around sporting events. They show some guy getting condemned to Hell and how it all could have been avoided.

Well, things couldn't have gotten any more awkward at that point.

Oh, except they did.

As quickly as the guy showed up, he was gone. The young man who was talking to us said, "I hate those guys."

"Christians, you mean?" I asked.

"Yes."

Well, great. That was not how I was hoping things would go.

"Listen," I said. "Perhaps my wife and I ought to leave. We are Christ Followers, and I am trying to listen to you and hear you out. But if that is how you feel about us, perhaps we should continue on our way." And with that, I turned to leave.

"No, wait!" he said. We turned back around. "I'm sorry. I didn't mean *all* Christians. I meant that guy. He follows me around and does that to me all the time."

"I understand," I said. And I can understand ill feelings toward an individual who treats you like you are invisible. Let me take a moment to say that I do not want to criticize the man with the tract. Would I try to witness to people in that way? No. But I am hesitant to criticize him. Deep down, his actions are driven by a desire to save souls, and that is at least admirable. I wouldn't do it that way simply because I don't think it is very effective. I've met a lot of Christ Followers, and none have told me they took on faith because of one of those tracts. Still, he was doing what he believed was his role in rescuing this world.

Okay, back to the story.

"Listen," the young man said. And now he looked dejected. His winsome personality was gone. He looked hopeless. "I'm asking people for forty dollars. That is what it costs for one of these counseling sessions that I mentioned. What do you say?"

I didn't know what to say. I was really torn. I felt like if I wrote him a forty-dollar check then I was endorsing that lifestyle. But I felt that saying no to him was flat out wrong. I wanted this young man to know that though I disagreed with his lifestyle, I still cared for him. I still loved him like I would if he didn't live that lifestyle. I wanted him to know a different kind of Christ Follower. I wanted to show him God's true nature, a nature that isn't clearly shown by ignoring him and passing a tract about Jesus to the people he is talking to.

"I really don't know how to respond," I told him honestly. "I just don't know if I can write you a check for your full amount. But here's what I know: I don't want to see kids get bullied. My wife doesn't want to see kids get bullied. God doesn't want to see kids get bullied, for their lifestyle choices or any other reason."

In my back pocket was a ten-dollar bill. It was the only cash I had. I pulled it out and gave it to him. "I have ten dollars on me. If you can use these ten dollars to help these kids to be treated right, I want you to have it."

I'm not sure I responded the correct way, but as I was talking to the young man, I kept thinking about my own kids. How would I want them to see me treat those who are different than me? I would want them to see the love for others that Christ displayed.

And the challenge of it all is to show that love while also maintaining faithfulness.

Chapter 11

December 2016

The Voice of God Project

12/1/16

For December, I will be reading Yann Martel's *The High Mountains of Portugal*, which was recommended to me by a close friend, Justin. He is possibly the most well-read person I know, and I highly value his opinion on books. I had told him that I was interested in reading *The Life of Pi*, another of Martel's works, but he had pointed me instead to *The High Mountains of Portugal*. I mentioned my love for *The Alchemist*, and he believed those two works to be very comparable.

12/17/16

One week to Christmas Eve. How hard to believe. It seems like only a couple of months ago I started on this journey, but now I am nearing its end. Another year of my life gone, another door closed. Speaking of doors closing, I have just recently exited the life stage of procreator thanks to my surgery yesterday.

Even though I know that I need to move on from that stage for a variety of reasons and that I'm completely content with the size of my family, it is hard to permanently shut that door. This is my last time forever to have a baby. Sarah is one month old today, by the way. It is going to fly by.

I don't exactly know what I'm trying to say. Perhaps it makes no sense. They told me to refrain from making any major life decisions or business deals for forty-eight hours due to the valium they gave me to cope with the pain of the surgery. Perhaps they should have told me to also refrain from journaling lest it become an undecipherable mess.

Sarah is an absolute beauty. I'm kicking myself already for not holding her enough or holding her and fiddling with my phone simultaneously. Why is it so hard to enjoy a wonderful, peaceful moment without being distracted? Distractions simply are wastes of life.

Why can't a moment filled with love, joy, peace, patience, kindness, goodness, gentleness, faithfulness, and self-control be enough? Why must we invite distractions that eat our fruit and leave us mere scraps? I feel like this is the question I should've been asking all year, and it's taken me till just now to figure that out. An answer appears to be hopeless. Only a dissertation can be offered.

We humans, regardless of faith, knowledge, background, or age, insist on wasting the most precious gift we have: life.

Craig Sager recently passed away, and I read some of his thoughts on life and time. That got me thinking about how the next day was Caleb's Christmas party at his school with his Kindergarten class, and even though I feel like I will never get caught up at work, I left the office and went to his party for a while. It was fun to see him in his school element. He had told Julie the day before that he wanted me to come to the party, and thanks in part to Craig Sager's wisdom about the fragility of time, I had decided that I would. How many opportunities will I have to do these things? How old do children get before they don't want their parents to come to their school Christmas parties? How many more years do I have in the Lebanon office so that my proximity allows me these opportunities? A kid was overheard by Julie to say he wished his parents could've gone to the party. I've been given a great gift, and I would be a fool to squander it.

The other day I was slowly falling asleep, but barely staying awake. My mind plays tricks on me when this happens. Anyway, I got the thought that love is like a flame. This was actually an extension of a thought from a few months back.

In one of Wilson's Wednesday night Bible classes, we talked about Genesis 12 and how God tells Abraham that He will bless him, and that Abraham will be a blessing and that in Abraham "all the families of the earth shall be blessed." In that way, blessing/love is like a flame passed from candle to candle. Think of the candlelight Christmas Eve singing you've probably found yourself participating in one time or another and how one candle is lit. And then from that one candle, the flame spreads to all the candles.

In the same way, Abraham becomes the candle from which all blessings originated.

But as I lingered in that state between being asleep and being awake, I felt like I could see the flame of love dancing and flickering in my mind's eye. And it occurred to me that I wanted to reach out and touch it. No, not touch it, just feel its warmth and cup my hand around it to keep the wind from blowing it out.

That is when I snapped awake. For it is in this way that I feel I am called to love my children.

They have this origin, this created character, this innocence, this natural ability to bless the world, and it is my responsibility as a father/parent to protect that spirit.

I am to care for my children while also remain concerned for them, and I have defined these actions in this way:

Care = spreading the flame.

Concern = protecting that flame.

12/23/16

I finished *The High Mountains of Portugal* on Tuesday, 12/20. Julie finished it today, and we had some time to discuss it. I did some digging online to see how other people translated Martel's message, and I'm pretty sure no one gets it. All the reviews I found are just summaries of the three stories that make up the book. Goodreads is worthless since it's just full of pretentious people that either declare that they totally got the book (with no evidence to prove it), or they pronounce the author stupid if they didn't understand it (and can't bring themselves to admit it). I found one lengthy review that briefly touches on faith but spends most of the time using the book to make political statements about natural resources. I'm not completely sure I understand the book, but I'm pretty dang sure the author of this article doesn't either.

Martel's novel is made up by three stories that stand alone, but the second two stories are impacted by the first. All three stories feature a chimpanzee that seems to symbolize faith in one way or another.

In the middle story, we see a mother who has lost a son many years prior and recently lost her husband, too. She explains how she and her husband handled the loss of their son differently. The husband obviously lived on the faith that God was taking care of his son, but I think the wife had more faith in the husband. She needed proof; he didn't.

My friend, Justin, put it like this: "He was making a statement of what we fill our life with. At the time of tragedy, we can be at peace or let it destroy us."

In the first story, we see an example of how a person can be destroyed. Tomas, who walks backwards since hit with the loss of his father, son, and wife, has found meaning only in exposing the lie he believes religion to be. His plan is to wreck faith for everyone; so, he travels all the way to the High Mountains or Portugal to do exactly that. He's willing to sacrifice his career, relationship with his uncle, and everything he has to accomplish this. But in the end, making this point is worthless.

He believes he has found something truly worthwhile, something that completely discredits God, and he points it out to a woman working at the church where this evidence exists. But the woman doesn't care. That's not what is bothering Tomas, though. What bothers him is how empty the entire thing is. He found his treasure and also found that it was not worth seeking. It does not make him feel any better. He has not gained his family back. He does not feel vindicated at all. In fact, when he gets back into the car to leave, it is the priest (or is it God Himself?) that he calls out to. Perhaps this first story is the most explicit example of Yann Martel's statement: "Life is a story; you can choose your story; a story with God is the better story."[2]

The Voice of God Project

The third story with Peter Tovy and Odo was my favorite one in the whole book. Odo is a chimpanzee that a widower named Peter Tovy adopts. He takes Odo to the High Mountains of Portugal to live with him.

I think Odo symbolizes God and how sometimes people may view your relationship with God as if you are hanging out with a chimpanzee. People cannot understand why a successful politician would give up his career and the luxuries of a first-world country to live in a shack in the middle of nowhere with no phone or electricity. Many times, when people come to faith, they see the world differently, and the world sees them differently. The goals of life become reprioritized. Achievements lose their luster. The race for success loses its meaning. A simpler, humbler way to live emerges. To outsiders, this makes us look strange. We may even appear to be devolving (the way Tovy felt he appeared to his sister), though we consider this to be a success (much like Tovy did).

Tovy is captivated by the presence of Odo. He can't always understand why, but he finds himself longing to be near the chimpanzee. He is always mindful of Odo's power, but he trusts Odo's goodness that he is safe around the chimpanzee.

Justin says it like this: "I think there is an underlying statement through the book that sometimes we can over-analyze instead of living for the day, and he uses animals to enforce that logic. Much like faith is better felt and experienced than trying to understand the reasons behind it."

I think Justin is exactly right, and it amazes me how common the theme of living in the moment has been throughout my 2016 spiritual journey. Think of *One Thousand Gifts* or *Zen and the Art of Motorcycle Maintenance*. But this theme was also prevalent in my month of prayer. It was the way that Viktor Frankl survived the holocaust.

It was the world prior to sin.

The following is my favorite excerpt from the book. It takes place in the third story when Tovy is on the phone with his sister, Teresa, who is trying to convince her brother to move back to Canada and has just accused him of being in love with his ape, Odo:

> Peter has learned the difficult animal skill of doing nothing. He's learned to unshackle himself from the race of time and contemplate time itself. As far as he can tell, that's what Odo spends most of his time doing: being in time, like one sits by a river, watching the water go by. It's a lesson hard learned, just to sit there and be. At first he yearned for distractions. He would absent himself in memories, replaying the same old movies in his head, fretting over regrets, yearning for lost happiness. But he's getting better at being in a state of illuminated, sitting-by-a-river repose. So that's the real surprise: not that Odo would seek to be like him but that he would seek to be like Odo.
>
> Teresa is right. Odo has taken over his life. She means the cleaning up and the looking after. But it's much more than that. He's been touched by the grace of the ape, and there's no going back to being a plain human being. That is love, then.[3]

I love how beautifully Yann Martel writes. And I believe (of course, I could be completely wrong) that he has captured the relationship of Christ and His followers. It is in such ways described above that Christ Followers should see the world differently, and thus, behave differently.

The sighting of the white rhino at the end of the book really stood out to Julie. This mythical rhino had been thought to be extinct with the occasional rumor of a sighting. No one knew for sure if it really existed, though. Except Peter. Thanks to Odo, he sees one and goes to his grave knowing the truth. But this white rhino spotting would never have happened unless he followed the path of Odo, a path that seemed random, unusual, and unnecessary, but was in reality completely intentional and meaningful.

This reminds me of another Peter. When Julie and I got married, we were very fortunate (thanks to my parents) to go on our honeymoon to Italy. When visiting Vatican City, the tour guide showed us an obelisk in the center courtyard of St. Peter's Basilica. He told us the story of how the obelisk once was the center of Nero's Circus, where a number of early Christ Followers were put to death for their belief.

The tour guide told us how Peter himself was killed at that circus. Peter refused to be crucified like his Lord; so, they crucified him upside down. The last thing he saw as he died was that obelisk.

The tour guide told us this story with all the confidence of any real, matter-of-fact story I'd ever heard. I was slightly embarrassed because I didn't remember that story in the Bible, but then I realized that it was part of Roman history, a completely different source.

It was that moment when my faith ownership really developed. I remember beholding that obelisk and having the thought that Peter was one of the only people in the history of the world to face the end of his life knowing beyond the shadow of a doubt whether or not Christ had risen.

I'm a logical person, and this made logical sense to me. If Peter had been making it all up, how could he have gone through watching his wife die before he also experienced a painful death? Would he go through that for a lie? What can give a person the resolve to face that experience?

Confidence. Assurance.

I know that John Ames in *Gilead* says not to look for proofs, and I agree that proofs are flimsy. But ever since seeing the object that Peter observed as his life drained out of his body, I have felt that I had experienced a proof of Christ's resurrection that has served me for years.

In the same way that Peter Tovy goes to his death knowing beyond the shadow of a doubt that the white rhino exists, Peter the disciple went to his death knowing beyond the shadow of a doubt that the risen Christ exists.

12/26/16

Christmas 2016 is over. If 12/25 is my favorite day of every year, 12/26 is definitely my least favorite. I hate the abrupt end to Christmas music and movies.

On Christmas Eve, Julie and I were talking in Sarah's room, and I told her I was sad about Christmas. She asked why, and I said because there are people here right now that won't be here in future Christmases. Her father turned 70 this year. I still have my paternal grandparents. We got to spend time with everyone in our extended families this year, which is rare because of all the various schedules involved. And with this being Sarah's first Christmas, it sure seems like it was a rare opportunity to celebrate Christmas with everyone still alive who is special to me.

I can't help but wonder might it be the last time? I'm already without my maternal grandparents, and Julie has no grandparents still alive. And even if this isn't the last time, it serves as a reminder that there will indeed one day be a last one.

I blame the kids and their recent infatuation with death for all of this…

12/29/16

I am rapidly approaching the end of this year. My conclusions to my spiritual journey have been heavy on my mind. I've had coffee or lunch with some good friends over the past two weeks (Justin, Nathan, Daniel, and Michael), and the conversations have been insatiable. Deep thoughts about life, the world, and God. I told Michael yesterday that I don't think I've changed over the past year, although I also don't think I'm the same.

Perhaps the best way to explain it is that I don't think I've changed in the way I expected. I kept trying to tell myself to seek peace rather than understanding, but in practice I couldn't help but seek understanding. And even though I knew better, perhaps this whole time I was still hoping that by understanding more, I would grow more love, joy, peace, patience, kindness, goodness, gentleness, faithfulness, and self-governance fruit in my life. But I didn't. I'm not sure I've grown in any of those areas. In fact, I've noticed the following paradox when you seek understanding:

When we think of one who has achieved a greater understanding of the world in which he/she lives (enlightenment, if you will), we always imagine these people to be at such peace. But what if when you began to understand the world, you didn't like what you learned? What if it reinforced the very uncomfortableness and awkwardness you hoped it would resolve? What if it only made you feel even more as if you don't belong here?

It reminds me of that lyric from *Under Pressure*, the Queen/David Bowie collaboration: "It's the terror of knowing what this world is about..."[4]

Understanding does not equate to peace. When will I understand that?

That being said, simply understanding that concept is so important because it is the necessary first step in determining how one will live, what they will base their life on, what they will strive for, what they will fill their life with, how they will go about achieving peace (or at least trying to). For no matter a person's background, I'm convinced that all people make it their goal in life to achieve peace. They may refer to it as happiness or joy or meaning or fulfillment, but whether they know it or not, they are actually referring to peace, that feeling of being on your death bed and being content with your life.

Chapter 12

Conclusion

The Voice of God Project

1/1/17

A year ago I started this journey, and now it is over. It was a unique year in which to do something like this. I should have known it was going to be an odd year early on when Peyton Manning was celebrating his Super Bowl victory on the sideline with Papa John. Little did I know how normal this would seem later when contemplating the crazy year in its entirety. It would be a year in which the Cubs would win the World Series, Bob Dylan would win the Nobel Prize for Literature, and Donald Trump would win the Presidency. One Cleveland professional sports team (the Cavs) would come back from a 3-1 series deficit to win a major pro sports championship, while another Cleveland team (the Indians) would give up a 3-1 series lead to lose a major pro sports championship. It was fitting that the 2016 World Series would be decided in extra innings of Game 7.

It was also a year of global unrest. Protests, movements, and violence became prevalent. Hate for each other and division sparked, and how to proceed became cloudy. Shootings, retaliations, and social media hate cloaked the country in fear. By order of the President of the United States, American flags were lowered to half-mast for fifty-four days during 2016 to honor the victims of various tragedies of violent nature or to honor the death of notable Americans.

I don't know that I've changed this year, but Julie told me that I have. She says my posture toward her is different, better.

Perhaps it is like swimming in my dad's pool at night. He has a light at the end of his pool, and I like to go under and see if I can swim the length of his pool without having to come up for air. Despite knowing better, I open my eyes under the water and watch the light as I swim. It's weird. Even though I know I'm getting closer to it, the light appears to get further away as I swim.

So maybe I've made progress even though life sometimes appears to contradict that. But I was expecting transformation. I was expecting to be dripping with patience. Why is my second-nature still to respond harshly rather than gently? Why does impatience remain my default? Why do I still worry and get anxious and let my thoughts steal my joy and peace?

Where do I go from here? I don't want to do like the disciples, who went back to being fishermen after Jesus was crucified, as if the three years spent with Him were meaningless (John 21:1-14). And yet I'm unsure about how to move forward. Doesn't one eventually get to a place where they just know? I saw that Ann Voskamp has a new book out, and I'm sure it's awesome. It took all I had to not buy it the other day since I was in the middle of *The High Mountains of Portugal*. But when I read the blurb about it, it starts talking about this way to live that is so right and good (and I'm sure it is), but it talks about it in a way that seems like there is a secret to it and that if you read the book you'll finally have this piece of information you are lacking. And then you will have a transformed life full of peace.

But don't you get to a point where you know all those secrets? Doesn't there come a time when you have to just *do*? Sometimes I'm guilty of just finishing a book, thinking it was great, putting it down, and moving to the next one.

But the spirit of *knowledge* isn't love, joy, peace, patience, kindness, goodness, gentleness, faithfulness, and self-control. The Spirit of <u>God</u> is. In other words, the more you know doesn't necessarily mean the more you grow (fruit). So how does one respond and where do I go from here?

As Lamar's favorite verse (Micah 6:8) puts it: "He has shown you, O mortal, what is good. And what does the Lord require of you? To act justly and to love mercy and to walk humbly with your God."

God has shown me what is good this year. And I am not given the burden that the fruit of God's Spirit must come easily to me. I am to be just and merciful. When I need to, I can be very intentional to respond to a situation in a way that bears the Spirit's fruit. If it doesn't come easily, that's okay. Because it's God's Spirit and not my own. Yes, I want to reflect that Spirit, but it doesn't mean I am not filled with God's Spirit just because it takes an intentional effort sometimes to be loving, joyful, peaceful, patient, kind, gentle, good, faithful, and self-governing.

The important thing is to remember that it's worth the effort. Perhaps intentionally replacing *my* spirit's fruit with God's is what it means to walk humbly with my God.

Finally, I have one more obligation: to recognize love, joy, peace, patience, kindness, goodness, gentleness, faithfulness, and self-control and to remember the source of that is God's Spirit. It may be embodied in someone who doesn't appear to have God's Spirit in his/her life, but I need to recognize that I am dealing with God in those moments, and to remember that He created us all, that we are in His image, and that His image (and our souls) bear this fruit.

My final conclusion regarding my year of reflecting on the fruit of the Spirit:

- Reading is Seeding
- Writing is Weeding
- Doing is Feeding

Writing in this journal has helped me to weed through my thoughts and make sense of them. Otherwise, they are just jumbled up, and they don't connect to anything that makes sense. But journaling allows the thoughts to develop. It allows me to pull out the weeds and focus on the fruit.

When I say feeding, I don't mean nourishing the garden (though perhaps that is applicable). I mean feeding myself with the fruit. After all, isn't fruit grown to be eaten? By intentionally acting in ways that are loving, joyful, peaceful, patient, kind, good, faithful, gentle, and self-governing, I am nourishing myself with the Spirit of God (even when doing so is difficult and not my gut reaction).

Conclusion

This makes so much sense; I don't know why it never occurred to me before. I was so worried about growing the fruit, that it never occurred to me that God grows the fruit so that we can partake of it. This fits so much better and more consistently with scripture. "Take and eat; this is my body" (Matt. 26:26). Jesus Himself uses this language. Even Jeremiah says, "When I discovered your words, I devoured them. They are my joy and my heart's delight, for I bear your name, O Lord God of Heaven's Armies" (Jeremiah 15:16).

Jeremiah devoured God's word. John says Jesus is the word (John 1:1). Paul says that the fruit I've studied comes from God's Spirit. So, I believe that by intentionally putting this fruit into practice, I can achieve the same thing Jeremiah achieves. I finally see why it is so important and why this fruit is more a gift of God instead of a way to measure how much of God's Spirit I have: They will be "my joy and my heart's delight," and I will "bear your name, O Lord God of Heaven's Armies".

It is exactly my goal to bear His name, which is where scripture comes into the discussion.

I've heard many people say that the Bible is no longer relevant because times are so different, but I couldn't disagree more. In fact, I think that time spent reading scripture would convince just about anybody that even though times change, people do not. And just because something is not addressed explicitly in scripture does not mean the text is invalid today. No, the point of the text is that we determine God's nature so that we understand how to live as His children in any situation.

Yes, the world has changed. But people have not. And God has not. And our mission has not.

God still speaks to us, but I believe we must be listening close enough that we hear not only the explicit communication but also the subtle, implicit messages.

If I can hear the voice of the one true God in all of the works I've read this past year, some of which are by atheists, Hindus, and other various backgrounds that don't all believe in Christ or practice His teachings, how can I not hear the voice of God in those people around me? Those that share life with me? Those that share the world with me?

Am I listening for the voice of God?

7/1/17

Six months later, and in the time since my last entry, I have taken my journal and made it into a book. I've told several people about my year of modern spiritual journey, and many times one question gets immediately asked. What was my conclusion? What did I learn?

I have had a difficult time putting my conclusion into words. When people asked me about it, I ended up talking about a certain part of my notes, or a quote from a book that I read. But none of that sufficed.

My conclusion was heavy on my mind. I couldn't put words to it. And then one night when I wasn't expecting it, my son helped me figure it out.

Usually, when I tuck Caleb and Lucy in at night, I read to them. However, on this night I decided not to read to them so I could get back into the living room and watch the Predators in the Stanley Cup Finals. I said a prayer with the kids and was about to leave. But then Caleb started asking me a bunch of questions about God.

Where is He? Where is Heaven? Why does God have so much power? How can He be everywhere at once? How do we know He's here in our presence?

All it takes to figure out how little you know about God is to get questioned by a kid who is longing for answers. I felt completely useless. I felt like I couldn't do my job as a father by answering my son's questions. He was depending on me for answers, and I seemed to have none! Most of our time was spent just listening to his concerns. His heart is already breaking for this world, just like mine during my spiritual journey. Caleb, at six years old, already sees injustice, and it bothers him as much as it does me.

We talked for over an hour, I missed the Stanley Cup game, and I felt like a failure as a parent. Caleb was basically asking me the same question others have been asking me. What is my conclusion? What have I learned? And I still couldn't find the words to help.

When your kids ask questions like he was asking me, you just want to answer them in a way that suffices your child's curiosity. You want them to feel sure in their faith, so that they can move through life and you never have to worry about them doubting God's existence and Christ's ability to provide salvation. You just want to check that box off the list of parenting to-do's so that faith is second-nature for your kids the rest of their lives.

But guess what. As I talked with Caleb, I realized that wasn't going to happen. And how wrong I was for trying to make that my goal! I love the way he wrestles with difficult things. I just want to stoke the flames of curiosity so that my children will remain curious, so that they will continue to pursue truth. Because I have faith that curiosity and pursuit will lead anyone straight to God and His son.

Faith isn't something to be figured out. God isn't someone that can be summed up in a conclusion. His will isn't simple enough to be contained in a formula. And our relationship with him can't be solved in an hour, a day, a month, or a year.

Being a Christ Follower is about forever. It's about allowing the mystery of God to enchant us. It's about pursuing Him and letting His wonder captivate us. It's about remembering what it was like to first be introduced to Him, what drew us to Him, what kept us up at night thinking about Him. It's about learning about Him slowly, gently, in a way that develops into this faith that can't be explained but is undeniable.

It's about willingness to crawl down into the abyss so that we can emerge on the other side, not perfect, but with our struggles, our doubts, our regrets, our wisdom, our meaning, our faith.

> "Let my cry come right into your presence God; provide me with the insight that comes only from your Word. Give my request your personal attention, rescue me on the terms of your promise. Let praise cascade off my lips; after all, you've taught me the truth about life! And let your promises ring from my tongue; every order you've given is right. Put your hand out and steady me since I've chosen to live by your counsel. I'm homesick, God, for your salvation; I love it when you show yourself! Invigorate my soul so I can praise you well, use your decrees to put iron in my soul. And should I wander off like a lost sheep – seek me! I'll recognize the sound of your voice."
>
> – Psalm 119:169-176 (MSG)

Acknowledgements

As I decided to turn this journal into a book, I've had numerous events happen that I cannot explain. People have gone out of their way several times to approach me and encourage me in some way or another. I can't list them all, but each of them are special to me. One that I must mention is my father, who read my book about a carpenter on his phone, and then went on and on about how much he liked it. And whether any of you realized it or not, your encouragement, just like his, served as motivation for me to finish this project. I hope I don't let you all down.

Of course, no one was as encouraging as my wife, Julie. She showed me what it means to support someone's dream. She encouraged me verbally several times, but it is her willingness for us to spend hundreds of dollars on graphic design, editing, ISBN numbers, websites, etc. on a book that potentially no one will read that really showed me how bought in she was. She was the one who sent me the Psalm 119 verse that so accurately describes my spiritual journey. I would be nothing without her.

To Caleb, Lucy, and Sarah, I want to thank you for letting your daddy have time to write. The three of you have humbled me as a person because I am so fortunate to have you in my life.

To the friends I have mentioned in this book, thank you for allowing me to include you by name in this work. There are a few other people that I must mention by name because they were such a vital part of my life as I wrote my journal and then later developed it into this book: Nathan Harris, Michael Pigg, and Wilson McCoy, who were a major part of my faith community while journaling; Todd Palmer, Matt Bean, Kevin Lee, and Jeff Brockette, who I spent many hours working with in 2016 and who have shaped me; Taylor Moore for editing this book and pushing me to make my writing better; Jessi Taylor for designing the Grassleaf Publishing logos; my friend, Mark, whose willingness to make time to review my project was very humbling; Samantha Wilson, Justin Harris, and Kevin Owen, who have encouraged my writing and whose opinions I highly value; and my parents, Brad and Janice Wagoner, and in-laws, John and Fay Kieffer for reading and encouraging my writing.

Finally, I want to thank you, the reader, for taking the time to read this work. If you found it worthwhile, I would appreciate you recommending it to a friend.

Notes

Foreword – Spiritual Journey Eve
1. Duncan, David James. *The River Why*. San Francisco: Sierra Club Books, ©1983. Print.

Chapter 1 – January 2016
1. Cron, Ian Morgan. *Jesus, My Father, the CIA, and Me: A Memoir…Of Sorts*. Nashville: Thomas Nelson, ©2011.
2. Cron, Ian Morgan. *Jesus, My Father, the CIA, and Me: A Memoir…Of Sorts*. Nashville: Thomas Nelson, ©2011, 201.
3. *Awakenings*. Dir. Penny Marshall. Perfs. Robin Williams, Robert De Niro. Columbia Pictures, 1990.
4. *Dead Poets Society*. Dir. Peter Weir. Perfs. Robin Williams, Robert Sean Leonard, Ethan Hawke. Touchstone Pictures, 1989.
5. Thoreau, Henry David. *Walden, or, Life in the Woods*. London: J.M. Dent, ©1908.
6. Whitman, Walt. *Leaves of Grass*. Philadelphia: David McKay, ©1900.

Chapter 2 – February 2016
1. Coelho, Paulo. *The Alchemist*. San Francisco: HarperSanFrancisco, ©1998.
2. Pirsig, Robert M. *Zen and the Art of Motorcycle Maintenance: An Inquiry into Values*. New York: Morrow, ©1974.
3. Lee, Harper. *Go Set a Watchman*. New York: HarperCollins, ©2015.
4. Lewis, C.S. *Surprised by Joy: The Shape of My Early Life*. New York: Harcourt, Brace, ©1955.
5. Pirsig, Robert M. *Zen and the Art of Motorcycle Maintenance: An Inquiry into Values*. New York: Morrow, ©1974, 208.
6. Ebert, Alex. *All is Lost – Original Motion Picture Soundtrack*. Community Music, ©2013.
7. Portman, Rachel. *The Cider House Rules – Original Motion Picture Soundtrack*. Sony BMG Music Entertainment, ©1999.

Chapter 3 – March 2016
1. Voskamp, Ann. *One Thousand Gifts: A Dare to Live Fully Right Where You Are*. Grand Rapids: Zondervan, ©2010.
2. Nouwen, Henri J.M. *The Way of the Heart: Connecting with God through Prayer, Wisdom, and Silence*. New York: Ballantine Books, ©1981.
3. Hudson, Trevor. *Holy Spirit, Here and Now*. Cape Town: Struik Christian Books, ©2012, 20.

4. Voskamp, Ann. *One Thousand Gifts: A Dare to Live Fully Right Where You Are*. Grand Rapids: Zondervan, ©2010, 61.
5. Voskamp, Ann. *One Thousand Gifts: A Dare to Live Fully Right Where You Are*. Grand Rapids: Zondervan, ©2010, 127.

Chapter 4 – April 2016
1. Irving, John. *The Cider House Rules*. New York: Morrow, ©1985.
2. Morricone, Ennio. "Vita Nostra." *The Mission: Music From The Motion Picture*. Virgin Records Ltd, ©1986.
3. *Awakenings*. Dir. Penny Marshall. Perfs. Robin Williams, Julie Kavner. Columbia Pictures, 1990.

Chapter 5 – May and June 2016
1. Dostoevsky, Fyodor. *The Brothers Karamazov*. Translated by Richard Pevear and Larissa Volokhonsky. New York: Everyman's Library, ©1992.
2. Dostoevsky, Fyodor. (2009). *The Brothers Karamazov*. Urbana, Illinois: Project Gutenberg. Retrieved July 23, 2017, from www.gutenberg.org/files/28504, 410.

Chapter 6 – July 2016
1. Robinson, Marilynne. *Gilead*. New York: Picador, ©2004.
2. *My Life*. Dir. Bruce Joel Rubin. Perfs. Michael Keaton, Nicole Kidman, Michael Constantine, Bradley Whitford, Haing S. Ngor. Columbia Pictures, 1993.
3. Robinson, Marilynne. *Gilead*. New York: Picador, ©2004, 210.
4. Hemingway, Ernest. *The Old Man and the Sea*. New York: Scribner., ©1952.

Chapter 7 – August 2016
1. Frankl, Viktor E. *Man's Search for Meaning: An Introduction to Logotherapy*. New York: Simon & Schuster, ©1984.
2. Frankl, Viktor E. *Man's Search for Meaning: An Introduction to Logotherapy*. New York: Simon & Schuster, ©1984, 84.
3. *Forrest Gump*. Dir. Robert Zemeckis. Perfs. Tom Hanks, Robin Wright, Gary Sinise, Sally Field, Mykelti Williamson. Paramount Pictures, 1994.

Chapter 9 – October 2016
1. Hall, Ron and Denver Moore with Lynn Vincent. *Same Kind of Different as Me: A Modern-Day Slave, an International Art Dealer, and the*

Unlikely Woman Who Bound Them Together. Nashville: W Publishing Group, an Imprint of Thomas Nelson, ©2006.
2. *The Mission*. Dir. Roland Joffe. Perfs. Jeremy Irons, Robert De Niro. Warner Bros, 1986.

Chapter 10 – November 2016

1. Vālmīki, and Ramesh Menon. *The Ramayana*. New York: North Point Press, ©2004.
2. *Inside the NBA*. NBA on TNT. TNT, Atlanta, 10 Nov. 2016.
3. Vālmīki, and Ramesh Menon. *The Ramayana*. New York: North Point Press, ©2004, 142.
4. Lloyd-Jones, Sally and Jago Silver. *The Jesus Storybook Bible: Every Story Whispers His Name*. Grand Rapids: Zondervan, ©2007, 2009.
5. Lloyd-Jones, Sally and Jago Silver. *The Jesus Storybook Bible: Every Story Whispers His Name*. Grand Rapids: Zondervan, ©2007, 2009, 17.
6. Vālmīki, and Ramesh Menon. *The Ramayana*. New York: North Point Press, ©2004, 491.
7. Vālmīki, and Ramesh Menon. *The Ramayana*. New York: North Point Press, ©2004, 396.
8. Hatmaker, Jen. "The politics of Jen Hatmaker: Trump, Black Lives Matter, gay marriage and more." Interview by Jonathan Merritt. *Religion News Service*. Oct. 2016. Online: religionnews.com/2016/10/25/the-politics-of-jen-hatmaker-trump-black-lives-matter-gay-marriage-and-more/

Chapter 11 – December 2016

1. Martel, Yann. *The High Mountains of Portugal: A Novel*. New York: Spiegel & Grau, an imprint of Random House, a division of Penguin Random House LLC, ©2016.
2. Martel, Yann. "Yann Martel Interview." Interview by Jennie Renton. *Textualities*. ©2005. Online: textualities.net/jennie-renton/yann-martel-interview
3. Martel, Yann. *The High Mountains of Portugal: A Novel*. New York: Spiegel & Grau, an imprint of Random House, a division of Penguin Random House LLC, ©2016, 300.
4. Mercury, Freddie, Brian May, Roger Taylor, John Deacon, and David Bowie. "Under Pressure." *Hot Space*. EMI Records, ©1982.

www.ingramcontent.com/pod-product-compliance
Lightning Source LLC
Chambersburg PA
CBHW020936090426
42736CB00010B/1160